T0248369

PRAISE FOR

THE MOTHER OF ALL SUCCESS MANUALS

"I hung onto Clara's words because she is a mom who has clearly been through the trenches. Reading this book felt conversational, like she was there with me, and I appreciate the action guides. This book helped me realize the cost of not being intentional in so many areas of my life."

—Leslie Lew, trauma-informed self-defense coach, mom of two

"From the moment I met Clara, I have been inspired. As an expert in boundaries and time management, I know the importance of efficiency and how to be in control of my time. Clara outlines key steps for Mompreneurs to regain time and create their own success! Whether you are an expert or starting from the beginning, this book will motivate and inspire you to be the best version of yourself!"

—Jen Potter, founder, EPIC 47, mom of three

"Clara's book is spot-on! So many working moms try to do it all. We can't help ourselves. I love her simple tips and practical approach—perfectly designed to help any working mom achieve more and be happy doing it."

—Christina Allyn, senior counsel, Boeing; chief counsel, Boeing Digital Solutions, Inc.; mom of two

"Pages into this book, I immediately knew this was a must-read. I feel confident saying Mompreneurs around the world are going to be so excited to get their hands on this book and will continue to feel empowered to have it all as Clara creates a true road map of what's possible for all of us."

—**Jes Landau,** national executive director and
founding leader, ONEHOPE Wine, mom of two

THE
MOTHER
OF ALL
SUCCESS
MANUALS

How to Control Your Days, Lose the Guilt,
& Find Harmony Between Work and Life

C L A R A   C A P A N O

AN INC.
ORIGINAL

This publication is designed to provide accurate and authoritative information in regard to the subject matter covered. It is sold with the understanding that the publisher and author are not engaged in rendering legal, accounting, or other professional services. Nothing herein shall create an attorney-client relationship, and nothing herein shall constitute legal advice or a solicitation to offer legal advice. If legal advice or other expert assistance is required, the services of a competent professional should be sought.

An Inc. Original
New York, New York
www.anincoriginal.com

Copyright © 2023 Clara Capano

All rights reserved.

Thank you for purchasing an authorized edition of this book and for complying with copyright law. No part of this book may be reproduced, stored in a retrieval system, or transmitted by any means, electronic, mechanical, photocopying, recording, or otherwise, without written permission from the copyright holder.

This work is being published under the *An Inc. Original* imprint by an exclusive arrangement with *Inc. Magazine*. *Inc. Magazine* and the *Inc.* logo are registered trademarks of Mansueto Ventures, LLC. The *An Inc. Original* logo is a wholly owned trademark of Mansueto Ventures, LLC.

Distributed by Greenleaf Book Group

For ordering information or special discounts for bulk purchases, please contact Greenleaf Book Group at PO Box 91869, Austin, TX 78709, 512.891.6100.

Design and composition by Greenleaf Book Group
Cover design by Greenleaf Book Group
Cover Images: ©ProStockStudio; Nevena Radonja. Used under license from Shutterstock.com

Publisher's Cataloging-in-Publication data is available.

Print ISBN: 978-1-63909-012-9

eBook ISBN: 978-1-63909-013-6

To offset the number of trees consumed in the printing of our books, Greenleaf donates a portion of the proceeds from each printing to the Arbor Day Foundation. Greenleaf Book Group has replaced over 50,000 trees since 2007.

Printed in the United States of America on acid-free paper

23 24 25 26 27 28   10 9 8 7 6 5 4 3 2 1

First Edition

TABLE OF CONTENTS

PREFACE

Growing up, I always felt as if something was wrong with me. It wasn't as if I didn't like children or didn't want children; I simply knew that I *also* wanted to work. And not just "have a job"—I wanted to run the show!

The idea of a big office—complete with chaos, a briefcase, and a paycheck—excited me. It was sexy, it was intriguing, and it was my dream.

I quickly realized, however, that even though it was OK for me to *have* the dream, I needed to temper it. I could dream . . . but only so big. When I would share my goals and big ideas, I always received comments such as:

"Well, that's nice, but you want a family, right?"

"How are you going to do all that and be a mom?"

"You'll change your mind once you have kids."

I began to realize that having a business *and* a family might not be a reality. But the dream never went away.

I was different from many other girls at that time because of my expectations. I always wanted and loved to work. I dreamed about the corner office, the business suits, and commuting to the office. Having a family was part of this dream, but I was OK if it never happened. That is not a knock on women who only wanted a family or those who never wanted a family. It's just for me, the dream of having a career was exciting and something I wanted to make happen. It's probably why I was a little older before I became a mom. Not only did I not find the "right" match until I was thirty, but I was also focused on building my reputation and business. And I was fine with that.

At the age of thirty-five, I became a mom. I didn't see thirty-five as too "old" to have a child. In fact, I do not know if I would have been as prepared to have a kid before then. It was a time of growth, excitement, fear, and hope. It is a chapter of life no one is prepared for, and you go into it with so many emotions, just praying to get it right and not screw up. Like most new moms, I was learning to maneuver through my new "life," trying to create a balance between work and motherhood for when I returned to my career. I was lucky because my husband at the time had a great job and I didn't need to go back to work . . . but I knew I would. I loved what I did, and having a child was not going to change that. I was confident that after twelve weeks of staying home with my son, I would have it all under control. I would then be able to go back to work strong and in control. Yeah, that was a nice dream.

Just three weeks after my son was born, I got the call. I was offered my dream job, the opportunity to oversee a large real estate office—the type of office I had *always* wanted to run. It was in the heart of the city, filled with high-producing real estate professionals, and the company had an amazing reputation. And it was gonna be *mine* to lead! There really was no decision for me. Of course, I would take it! Together, my husband and I would figure it out; he and I would arrange the details of how to balance new parenthood and work. It would be fine. But it wasn't.

As I shared my excitement with others, I was met with very opposing reactions. Comments like:

"You will regret this."

"How can you put your career before your son?"

"Your husband has a good job. Why do you have to work?"

And those comments were not just from strangers. Many were from those closest to me. I was floored.

I didn't understand. And more so, I could not understand why others didn't understand. Why were they questioning my abilities and dedication? Why was I not getting support? I *loved* my new son, and I would continue to be a *great* mom; why couldn't I do both? Why was it that if the position was offered to my husband, there would have been a celebration, but for me there was anger, shame, and disapproval?

So, with little support, I moved forward and took the job. And it was hard. Really hard. Harder than I expected. I cried on the way to work. I was sleep deprived. My relationship with my husband became strained. My son would cry when he had to leave his nanny and come back to me. It was awful. But it still was not a mistake.

When I later became a single mom, I continued on my path. I put myself through a master's program, changed careers, and did my best. Through it all, there were many breakdowns, but also times of great happiness. I accomplished a lot and was dedicated to letting others know that hard work and motherhood could coincide.

Fast-forward to the present. I have a thriving career that I love, and my son, now sixteen, and I have a great relationship. As a trainer, speaker, and business coach, I do travel quite a bit, but we work it out. However, I have realized that the perception of me as a "Mompreneur" has not changed much in society's eyes. When I am on the road teaching for the business sales training system Ninja Selling, speaking at conferences, or delivering my own Success Workshops, one of the first questions people ask is, "So, who takes care of your son when you're on the road?" And this question does not get asked once, but several times at each event. Even more interesting, my male counterparts with children *never* get asked this question. It begs the question *why?*

Many great fathers/husbands/second parents do an *amazing* job at taking care of their kids while "Mom" is away, but society still has the default perception that Mom is the go-to. Mom is the first person the school calls when the kids are sick; Mom is the one that needs to bake cookies for the class and change her schedule to attend field trips. And you know what? We moms *get it done!*

Writing this book brought me back to life. I was tired of feeling bad for loving my job and for wanting to do more. I was always trying to defend my decisions and felt I had to qualify every conversation with "but I do love my kid." It was almost as if society made you feel and appear as less of a mother if you enjoyed working outside of the home—like you were abandoning your "real" duties.

Writing this book connected me not only with my goals, but also with an incredible community of Mompreneurs. It reminded me how passionate and beautiful we are as strong-minded women, and how we have to let our light and voices shine. No more holding back. As I began researching this book and spoke to other Mompreneurs, I realized several things:

1. We need help.

2. There are more of us struggling than I thought.

3. We need real tools, not just cheerleaders. We don't have time for fluff.

4. We have to support each other.

5. We have to be vulnerable and ask for help. Yeah, that's a big one.

Writing this book has taught me that we still do have to make choices; maybe we cannot have it all today, but we *can* still have it all. It may simply take time.

INTRODUCTION

What *is* a Mompreneur? In my opinion, she is strong, passionate, hardworking, and wants to help make the world a better place. She loves her career and her family. She has a thirst and drive that allows her to accomplish more in one day than most do in an entire year. She is not without flaws, but is confident and aware that she is a better business owner, mother, wife, friend, and more by learning how to find the harmony in making it all work and showing others that you can have both a thriving professional and a full personal life at the same time.

As a Mompreneur, you tackle many things each day: You take care of your business, clients, staff, and projects, and then return home to take care of all the demands there as well. You may have assistance at home, while others may not. Regardless, at the end of the day, many of life's demands fall on your shoulders. The truth is: We are all a hot mess. We screw up. We fail. We do the best we can. And that is wonderful! We are wonderful.

The reality is that Mompreneurs are *awesome*, and we need to let the world see us, appreciate us, and allow us to shine. We must share our messages and talents.

There are many resources that support women and moms; they offer ideas and concepts for empowerment and habits, but there are few that provide real tools that the Mompreneur can implement to see immediate change and progress.

I want to help Mompreneurs with the *how* in creating their goals. The changes that working moms make will impact generations and will bring us professional women closer as a community and sisterhood. As we share our voices, stories, and challenges, we will bond and let go of the loneliness we often feel as working mothers. This book will change lives—and not just for you, the Mompreneur who reads it, but for everyone you touch. Yes, it will help you in business, but more important, it will help you live a better life. We are all connected, and as we work to improve ourselves and our lives, we also improve the lives of our families, friends, and clients.

This book will help you develop healthy boundaries, communicate effectively in both business relationships and relationships on the home front, create a foundation for self-care, realize the power of your vision and how to communicate it, and establish a mindset to keep you focused, purposeful, and passionate. My hope is that this book will help you unleash your talents. It will call you to be unapologetic in pursuit of your dreams. And it will help you be unstoppable in working toward your goals. It will give you the tools to take back control of your mindset, your time, and your business so you can find that harmony between work and personal life. My hope is that this book brings you peace, allows you to know you are enough, and reinforces that you are a *great* Mompreneur who can accomplish anything!

I don't want this book to be just another motivational piece. This book will be a guidebook to success. It is a manual that provides real tools, concepts, and skills to help Mompreneurs maneuver through the challenges and obstacles of daily life, both at home and in the workplace. I want you, the Mompreneur, to know that having a successful life and business *can* be done. I want to provide you with support when you feel like you're alone and want to give up.

I have divided this book into three sections: Mindset, Skill Sets, and Action Goals. Each section highlights the skills and tools of real-life Mompreneurs and how they put these practices in place, and each chapter ends with action steps to help you create your own plan. I want to support you in taking these simple concepts and putting them into action in a way that will work for you. I do not want you to simply read the book; I want you to *engage* with it and apply the concepts so that real change can happen. Again, this is a guidebook and a road map for success, not just a book to motivate you. This book will tell you what to actually do!

This book is also a celebration of you, the Mompreneur. The ladies who give their all each and every day, chasing their dreams of being strong, independent businesswomen *and* amazing, loving, and giving moms. This book is for you, to help you, to guide you, and to let you know you are OK, you are loved, and you are honored. Cheers to you, Mompreneurs! Cheers to your strength, your light, your passion, and your commitment to give your all! Stand back world—here you come!

SECTION 1

MINDSET

The Key to Unlocking Success

1

MINDSET OF A
CHAMPION MOMPRENEUR

*I really think a champion is defined not by their wins,
but by how they recover when they fall.*

—SERENA WILLIAMS

Each day we have a choice. We can choose to be a player or a victim. A player shows up with purpose, focus, and an intention to succeed. A victim does just the opposite. They are defeated, cast blame, and give their power to others.

A champion is a player that takes it to an even higher level. When we are a champion, we don't just show up with positivity and purpose, we also show up with determination and grit. We show up with the resolve to never give up, even in the face of adversity.

World-class skier Lindsey Vonn exemplifies what it means to be a champion. She has been named as one of the best female skiers in the world *and* she did all of this while facing two career-ending injuries. She fell . . . she fell a lot. In fact, just a few months before the Olympics, she was injured so badly she was told she would never be able to compete. But she did compete, and she *won* the gold medal. As a champion, she continued to get up and keep going. Champions understand that the road to greatness is not easy and there will be challenges, but they face those challenges and keep going.

Mompreneurs are natural champions; we are strong, determined, and show great courage, even when under pressure. But like all people, we can sometimes fall from a champion mindset. Our desires to help and be there for others can overwhelm us and pull our focus away from the things we need to focus on. Many Mompreneurs think that multitasking and "doing it all" are what make a champion when, in reality, it is those types of actions that detract from a champion mindset. Part of being a champion is having the courage to stand up and face adversity. Sometimes that means (and requires) that a Mompreneur says *no* to items that will not fit into or support her overall goals. Being a champion is not about being there for others; it is about making the right choices when necessary so you can show up, focus, and serve at your greatest level.

When you choose to be a champion in life, you take control over your personal success. And I am here to help you become a champion, take control, and become the Mompreneur you are destined to become.

Being a champion is a daily commitment. Not that we must be one every day, but that is the goal. When you lay a foundation and work your best each day, you will create the habits of a true champion. Greatness lies in the small actions we take each day; when you set up your day as a champion, that is what you will become. Here are some of the ways you can develop the mindset of a champion:

PROGRAM YOUR BRAIN FOR SUCCESS

Our brains are computers. We program them regarding what to look for and what to expect. One of my favorite sayings is "What you focus on expands." We become who we believe we are. Therefore, we need to make sure our brains are set up with the belief system that matches the outcomes we desire. The biggest challenge for Mompreneurs is that we worry . . . a lot. For many, if we could get paid for worrying, we would be billionaires! We worry about our families, our jobs, others, money, the pets . . . the list goes on and on.

Here is something you need to consider: If the brain is a computer and it is set to focus on what we tell it to, and if we are constantly worrying, then . . . well, our focus will always be worry. John Assaraf and Murray Smith said in their book *The Answer*, "Worry is a prayer for things we do not want."[1] Now that is *powerful*. When we worry, we are praying for what we *do not want*.

When we worry about kids getting sick, we are sending out that message to the universe.

When we worry about not having enough money, time, energy, we are sending out that message to the universe.

When we worry about failing, yup, you guessed it, we are sending out that message of failure to the universe (or the greater energetic realm).

In fact, we get what we expect. And if we expect what we worry about, that is exactly what the world will give back to us.

One of the best ways to escape from constant worry is to practice daily written affirmations. Begin by choosing to start a positive habit or accomplish a certain goal. Here are some examples of positive affirmations:

- I enjoy earning $X a year or more.

- I live with purpose and passion.
- I am limitless and unstoppable.
- I am a world-class Mompreneur.
- I am fit, healthy, and energized every day.

Once you have your statement, write it down twenty-five times each day. That's right: Write it down. Studies suggest that repeating positive affirmations to ourselves can help us respond in a less defensive and resistant way when presented with life challenges. They are a mental health tool that can help you develop a healthy sense of self and build a more resilient brain.[2] As you write your statement, the message begins to imprint on the nonconscious part of your brain, effectively telling your brain, "This is who I am." Each day, writing your statement will begin to reprogram your brain and start the process of creating this vision internally, which will then spill outward. For some, this exercise might seem unusual and outside of the box.

I was one of those people when I was introduced to affirmations in 2009. At first, I thought it was a little strange and uncomfortable, but I agreed to do it and the results have been amazing. Some of my affirmations have included the following:

- I motivate and inspire others to greatness daily.
- I show love to my family daily.
- I am present and purposeful in all I do.

As a coach, I see the impact this simple daily exercise has on my clients and colleagues. It really does work. For instance, one of my Mompreneurs was *very* skeptical of the affirmation exercise. Chantel wanted to increase her income so she chose to use an income goal for her affirmation. This income goal was higher than anything she had made in the past. She had a limiting belief around her ability to earn a six-figure income and didn't believe she could accomplish that goal, but with my encouragement, she began her practice, and every day for a year, she wrote down her goal. By the end of that year, she had exceeded her goal by $1,500! She has continued her affirmations and has seen success follow each year. She tells me (and others) that her time of daily affirmations helps her stay focused and grounded; it allows her to reach her goals and is one of the most important parts of her day.

As I mentioned, when I first was introduced to the idea of written affirmations, I was skeptical. I was attending a four-day Ninja Selling Installation (a program that changed my life; I would eventually become a Ninja Selling coach and instructor), and when we got to the portion where we were writing affirmations, I thought they were weird and a waste of time. But I did it because I had committed to following through. The first year, I chose an income goal; it was larger than what I had ever made, but I knew it was possible if I worked hard. Every day for that year, I wrote that goal down, and like Chantel, I exceeded my goal. I became a believer! I have since continued to incorporate affirmations into my daily routine. I am now focused on a behavioral goal rather than income. My current affirmation is: "I motivate and inspire others to greatness daily." I chose this focus because, at my core, that is who I truly want to be.

What about you? Who do you want to become? Affirmations can be whatever you want; they should simply represent a goal of becoming the version of yourself you know you can be. It can be a physical statement: "I enjoy weighing 125 pounds" or "I am fit and healthy at 125 pounds." It can be behavioral: "I enjoy arriving five minutes early to all appointments." Or as shown previously, an income goal: "I enjoy earning/I enjoy receiving $X."

Affirmations work. They will not only impact your success at work, but can also help do the following:

- Raise your confidence before an important event or meeting
- Diminish negative feelings such as anxiety, anger, or impatience
- Increase your self-esteem
- Find the motivation to keep going
- Improve your level of productivity
- Quit a bad habit

Written affirmations are simple ways to connect with your vision and program your nonconscious brain for success. We become what we think, we create what we expect, and we act in accordance with our internal programs. I encourage you to try it for thirty days. Again, what you focus on expands. Put your focus into being a champion.

BE YOUR BEST DAILY

We've all had a moment when we felt on top of the world. I refer to this as being "in the zone." It could last for a day or longer. Ask yourself, "Who am I when I am in the zone?" Then list five words you would use to describe yourself during this time. My words are confident, purposeful, energized, present, and authentic. This is me when I am at my best. Showing up as this version of myself is my job. It is what my clients expect of me and the commitment I have made to them.

Every morning before my workday begins, I check in with this vision of my best self to make sure that as I prepare for the day, I am setting myself up to become this person. My mission is all about serving others; I cannot provide the best service to others if I am not at my best.

Now let's be real for a moment. Life happens, and I do not always wake up as this person; I am not always energized, prepared, and feeling inspired. But I have to be for my people. So what do I do when I am not yet there? I take control with a few steps to help me move into this zone. For example, if I am not feeling energized, I may go for a walk and get some fresh air, listen to some music (classic Madonna and The Go-Go's work well for me), or just get up and stretch. If I am not prepared, I will look over my notes and take a few moments to visualize how I want my next call or training to go. And if I need some inspiration, I have a few mentors that I look to for a pick me up, including Brené Brown, Mel Robbins, Robin Sharma, and Prince Ea.

Get clear on who you are at your best and create a standard and expectation to be that person every day.

GROW YOUR MIND EACH DAY

One of the best ways to transform into a champion is to have a growth mindset. In her book *Mindset*, Dr. Carol Dweck illustrates the importance of a growth mindset, a mind that is open to learning and failure. She states that in her studies, all champions showed a growth mindset; they all had a willingness to learn daily, to expand their current knowledge, and to reach outside of their comfort zone.[3]

Here are two simple ways to develop a growth mindset:

- Read daily. As little as ten minutes a day can help to expand your mind and teach you new things.

- Listen. Talk with people and listen to them. We learn by listening. People are fascinating so take time to grow relationships.

To expand on listening, remember that podcasts are free and cover topics from self-help to business, leadership, healthy living—the list is endless.

If you want success, you must have the mindset to support you. It does not take a lot of effort but will require you to make the choice to show up and make it happen. Choose to be a player; choose to be a champion of your life and business. It is a game changer.

ACTION STEPS

1. On a scale of 1–10, where are you currently as far as showing up as a champion? _____

2. What is one thing you can do to get closer to a 10?

   _____

   _____

   _____

   _____

   _____

3. Choose an affirmation to work on for the next thirty days (or longer).

   _____

   _____

   _____

   _____

   _____

4. Who are you when you are at your best? What are
your five words?

_____

_____

_____

_____

_____

5. Biggest aha moment from this chapter:

_____

_____

_____

_____

_____

2

BEING PURPOSEFUL AND PRODUCTIVE

As a working mother, I know that women can be both
professionally ambitious and deeply committed to their families.

—TORY BURCH

As a business coach and strategist, I study successful people all day long. I pay attention to what they do—and even what they don't do—as I know I can learn from their successes and struggles. In studying successful Mompreneurs, I have found that there is a difference in how they do things, show up, and execute their days. There is a mindset and a belief system successful Mompreneurs develop to help them face the obstacles of their days. A thriving Mompreneur has learned it is about running her days with purpose and focus. She has realized how to use her talents, skills, and knowledge to become the CEO of her business and her life.

So what does it mean to be a productive and purposeful Mompreneur? There are several objectives a Mompreneur must master:

- Be strategic with your week.

- Have passion.

- Delegate.

- Lead by example.

- Ask for help.

- Practice self-care.

Let's dive into each of these and learn more about what it takes to be a successful Mompreneur.

BE STRATEGIC WITH YOUR WEEK

The successful Mompreneur knows that the week starts before Monday even arrives. Success comes from planning the week before it begins, so she is purposeful in how she approaches her days. Before her week starts, she spends time getting her plan together and defining how she will use her time, who she needs to meet with or follow up with, and other operational expectations. She must prepare in advance, otherwise the distractions of the week will take control and she will be reactionary rather than purposeful. What a seasoned Mompreneur knows is that she is not just preparing for the workweek, but also for the personal week. Remember, a Mompreneur is a CEO at the office and also at home.

A great example of a brilliantly strategic Mompreneur is someone close to me whom I greatly admire. Yes, my mom. She was the first Mompreneur I knew, and she has taught me several lessons (even if I never let her know that).

My mom, Sandra, was a master at planning the week and getting all her ducks in a row. I can still visualize her menu plan for the week; each day, she had written down what we would be having for dinner. Monday: chicken, broccoli, rice, salad. Tuesday: tacos, refried beans. Wednesday: pot roast, potatoes and carrots, salad. This not only helped her save time, but she then knew how to shop. In addition, she also could anticipate the feedback from the family and be ready to tell us, "Tough. Eat it or make your own meals." In her own sweet way, of course.

Another clever thing she did after planning her schedule at the beginning of each week was to share it with my dad; together, they would discuss what was happening with work, the kids, and other obligations. This discussion allowed them to know the other's plans for the week so they could work together to make sure all items were covered. So simple and so efficient. They would address who would take the kids to school and who would be home at what time, if there were evenings one needed to work, et cetera.

I asked my mom why she always did this and her answer was simple: The weekly plan helped to alleviate stress for the entire family, it allowed her to mentally prepare for the week, and it saved her time. Of course, with four kids and a husband, that didn't mean she never deviated from the schedule, but the plan gave her direction and gave her the ability to know how to get back on track if she was pulled off.

As a result, I plan my weeks too. Many scheduling tools are available, and you can find one that works for you. You might be tech-savvy and want to be able to update and share your Google calendar, or old school and want to put pen to paper in a bound weekly organizer, or maybe you prefer a giant whiteboard or calendar in your kitchen for everyone to access. The beauty is that you can use what will work best for *you*.

My mom was able to keep it all in her head, but I need to write it down. I use a simple written planner for my weekly business plan.

I carve out thirty minutes each Sunday evening and prepare for the week ahead. I reflect on the previous week, set my targets for the current week, and plan my schedule, including time off. I coordinate and synch my schedule with my computer so that it all works together, and I have my calendar on the go. It is easy and makes me purposeful even before the week begins. Here is the basic weekly schedule that I follow—I go into more detail on how to develop your own plan in later chapters (and you can find a weekly success planner in the Appendix).

5:15 a.m.: Wake up/gratitude/walk; listen to podcast

6:00 a.m.: Affirmations/visualization/note cards/review schedule for day

6:30 a.m.: Make breakfast for son

7:00 a.m.: Be at desk ready for appointments

(I take a break every ninety minutes.)

11:30 a.m.–1:00 p.m.: Nap (forty-five minutes is my sweet spot)

1:00–3:00 p.m.: Appointments*

3:00 p.m.: Get son from school; make calls in car

3:30–6:30 p.m.: Time with son; make dinner

6:30–7:30 p.m.: Close out day/reflection; prepare game plan for next day

*Note that I schedule personal activities such as exercise during my appointment times.

HAVE PASSION

As we discuss in chapter 3, a purposeful Mompreneur is clear on her passion both in business and life. She is focused on providing value at a high level, and she uses her passion to drive her. She knows that not every day is filled with rainbows and unicorns, but her passion keeps her moving forward. It is the rocket fuel that gets her up and going each day. Passion is different for each person. A person's passion may be family, financial freedom, the ability to travel, or simply the work itself. Often the areas will blend together as we are driven by all areas.

Carrie's passion was and still is her family. She wanted a career and business that would allow her to make a good living and also have the flexibility to be there for her family. Because of this, she acquired a passion for flexibility. When I met Carrie, we became fast friends in addition to working together professionally. Her kids were young, eight and ten. Her flexible schedule allowed her to be present for every school field trip and meeting, be home if one of her kids was sick, and be able to take vacations. It was Carrie's passion for flexibility and family that drove her. On the tough days, she would stop to think about what other career could give her such flexibility to be available for her family, and then realize she had it pretty good. Her passion for family drove her to push harder so she could have continued flexibility and control over her schedule. Now that her kids are grown, she has maintained her passion for flexibility and this affords her the ability to travel, spend more time with her husband, and have the time to simply enjoy life on her terms and schedule.

My passion has changed over the years. When I was young, I wanted to make money. I wasn't married and didn't have a child, so building my wealth was a driver. After my son was born, my passion was more about stability and flexibility; being able to provide for him as a single mom and be there when he needed me were the most important things. Now that he is older, my passion has turned to contribution and legacy: How can I leave a mark and message to help others?

When it comes to your passion, there is no right or wrong answer; your passion is *your* passion. It is what drives you to be your best and to show up on both the good and the rough days. It is what brings you focus, energy, and determination. Without passion, we get lost and lose the energy needed to build greatness and become the person we know we can be, for us and for our families.

DELEGATE

You cannot do it all. No one can, not even the best of the best. A successful Mompreneur must learn it is not about doing it all; it is about identifying the right things and doing those at a high level. If you try to do too much, you will get distracted from your main vision and purpose, and your business and personal life will suffer.

As a busy mom of two boys, Maria had her days packed. Because she was such a dedicated and gifted real estate agent, her business grew quickly. On top of that, her sons played competitive sports. She wondered how was she going to serve her clients, the demands of her growing business, *and* be there for her kids. She would have to delegate.

Delegation is a struggle for many Mompreneurs. Maybe we feel guilty about not doing it all, or we just don't think others can do it as well as we can. Perhaps a little of both. Regardless, many fight this component until they realize they have to surrender to it in order to create their vision. The honest truth we all have to face is that we *cannot* do it all.

Not doing it all doesn't make us weak, in fact, it does quite the opposite. It allows us to focus our time in the right places and with the right people.

The honest truth we all have to face is that we *cannot* do it all.

Maria learned this after she hired an assistant. She was then able to focus on her clients and family and let her assistant help with paperwork and other administrative tasks. Of course, she was capable of doing *all* of those items, but she just knew that was not where she should be spending her time.

For me, delegation often comes in the area of housework. I hate it, and I am not good at it. So now I hire it out. I have a cleaning company come weekly for just a couple of hours. In addition, I have someone that can help me walk the dog and do mailings, and as soon as my son gets his license, he can manage duties with the car such as getting gas and taking it for servicing.

In the beginning, delegating was challenging for me; I wasn't making a lot of money and had a lot of guilt. "Who am I to have an assistant? Other moms can handle all of these tasks. Why can't I? I really shouldn't spend the money." However, once I made the decision (which took me about six months and came at the urging of my mother, who always knows better), I quickly learned it was the right thing for me to do. I was able to delegate items that I, quite frankly, didn't enjoy to people who could do it better than me and then use that time to reinvest back into my business, my clients, and *my life*. I was much happier, had less stress, and ended up increasing my business because I was investing my time and focus on the right things.

LEAD BY EXAMPLE

We must understand that others are watching us. Some people are looking for clues on how they can grow and improve, and others (sadly) are waiting and watching for us to screw up. We need to have grace and confidence to show up and be the person we want to be.

It is important that we think about the messages we are sending by how we show up. For me, it is critical to be a good role model for my son, so I think about the lessons I need to model for him:

- I say I am sorry and take ownership when I make a mistake.

- I never give up. When I fall down, I get back up.

- I follow through on my word.

- I work hard.

- I laugh and show love daily.

I want to make sure my actions connect with these messages. And for my Mompreneurs, here are some behaviors to model in your own life:

- Ask for help when you need it.

- Do not worry about being perfect.

- Laugh at yourself.

- Help others.

- Be kind and also hold true to yourself.

If I want others to understand and see that these actions can work, I need to make sure I model it for them. So, on the days I do not want to get up, I must so I can model what I teach. When I am feeling guilty, I need to stand up and show love for myself. When I want to be lazy, I need to reconnect and get focused.

If I do not follow and practice what I teach, I am not being the role model my Mompreneurs need. I am not being who I need to be to serve and help others. One of my affirmations is that I motivate and inspire Mompreneurs to greatness daily. How can I do that if I do not lead by example?

Think about who you are serving, who are you showing up for, and how can you model that behavior and message for them.

ASK FOR HELP

I am not sure why, but for some reason many moms struggle with asking for help. Messages from society, our families, and others we see have created this paradigm where if we ask for help, we are somehow showing the world we are failing, we are not perfect, and we are less deserving of love and praise for all we are doing.

I fell into this trap after my son was born. Before I had him, it was easier to "do it all," but after he was born, I completely crumbled. Within the first month of having a newborn, I was offered a promotion at work (which I took) and developed postpartum depression. Now a "smart" Mompreneur would have called a time-out and asked her family and office team for help, but I was not a smart Mompreneur yet.

So every day I woke up at 4:30 a.m., took my son for a walk, and then got in the car for my fifty-minute commute (during which I cried the whole way for about four months). I worked until 5:00 p.m., made another fifty-minute commute, and then arrived home to make dinner and be Mom. All with a *huge* smile on my face to show everyone "I got this." I was fearful that if I let them know what was going on behind the curtain, they would think less of me, they would lose trust in me and my ability to lead them, and I would be a huge disappointment. That fear only grew and eventually caused my world to come crumbling down.

Within about eight months, I was on notice at work that my performance was not on par with what they needed, my team was sharing their thoughts on my being a poor leader, I was not present with my son, and I was on the verge of divorce.

Why couldn't I just ask for help? Why couldn't I just let people know I was hurting and scared and overwhelmed? Oh, that's right . . . guilt and shame.

I had to have a real conversation with myself about my situation, but I also talked with some of my very close friends, where I learned that *all of us* felt this way. *What??* We all felt like this? We *all* had feelings that we were failing and doing it all wrong? What an eye-opener.

My friends shared their stories and I began to learn I wasn't alone. I saw that they got through it by being honest and asking for help. They told others what they needed and even used the strategy of delegation to assist them in what needed to get done. They taught me that asking for help was not a weakness, but a strength; it showed others that you could take control and know your limits.

Asking for help was challenging at first, mostly because I didn't know where and how to do it. But soon it became easier. Now, it is not nearly as hard. I have no problem asking my friend to pick up my dog if my plane is delayed. I can ask my sister to help with picking up my son, and I can ask my team to do things at work. I do not need to do it all, and these people are happy to help. (Please note that they also can ask for help from me and I am there when they need me too.)

Hillary Clinton once wrote that it takes a village, and it does. Learning how to ask for help saved me. It taught me to forgive and love myself for what I can do and also for the things I cannot do. It taught me that it is OK to not be perfect and to embrace the notion that I am perfectly imperfect.

PRACTICE SELF-CARE

This is one of the most important lessons I have learned. Top Mompreneurs take care of themselves. They eat right, exercise, and get sleep. And they do this not for their ego but rather to serve others better. They know that to help others (through their business and in their family), they need to be in good health and have energy. You cannot take care of others or show up prepared, focused, and energized for your business if you are sick, run-down, and exhausted. In her book *Thrive*, Arianna Huffington shared the detrimental effects of sleep deprivation, when she described her collapse at work from exhaustion.

One of my favorite examples of self-care comes from my friend Karen. Karen is a successful businesswoman and the mother of five (yes, five!) boys. Her manager noticed that once a week, Karen would disappear for about two and a half hours. When she asked her where she went, Karen responded with a smile, "I was at the movies." Yes, Karen would take time for herself each week and go to a movie by herself. As an independent contractor, Karen had the flexibility to build her own schedule. She used this time to get herself centered, reflect, and get some overall peace and quiet. She told me that this was incredibly important to her and her business; she needed that time to herself. She holds firmly that those few hours away also made her a better mom and wife.

I learned a lot from Karen, and because of her success in this area, I work hard to block time for my personal space each week. I schedule walks by myself and often reserve at least one day a month just to myself where I watch TV, read, or just sleep. This is my recharge day.

Many working moms believe that taking breaks for themselves is selfish or that there simply isn't time for it. We need to reprogram that belief system. Self-care is *not* selfish! In fact, it is just the opposite. The more we care for ourselves, the better our results will be, and the more our business (and family) will thrive. You may not be an independent contractor like Karen, but you still can build in time for yourself. Maybe it is asking for an extended lunch hour or to leave early one day; you could ask for a couple of hours on the weekend or one evening. You may have to get creative—and you *will*. Taking time for yourself is critical and needs to be a priority.

Being a successful Mompreneur demands a lot. We need to show up differently than others, and we need to pay attention to what it takes to achieve success. We are all CEOs. Whether we run our own company or work for another, we are still the CEO of our division, our team, our lives. Top Mompreneurs understand this. Let's learn from them how to be strategic with our weeks, have passion, delegate, lead by example, ask for help, and practice self-care. When we follow these points, we can develop the mindset of a smart Mompreneur and grow into the businessperson and human being we know we can become.

ACTION STEPS

1. What is one thing you can delegate?

_____

_____

2. Who can you delegate this to?

_____

_____

_____

_____

3. Who is someone you can get support from? What can they help you most with right now?

_____

_____

_____

_____

_____

4. Who is another woman you admire? What is it that they do/have done that impressed you? How can you learn from them?

_____

_____

_____

_____

_____

5. Biggest aha moment from this chapter:

_____

_____

_____

_____

3

CREATING YOUR VISION

I was once asked what could be worse than being blind.
I said to have sight but no true vision.

—HELEN KELLER

Most people go through life merely existing—going through the motions but having no real vision of where they want to go or why it is important. But a person with a strong vision can accomplish great things, and creating that vision can help a person gain clarity on their path. Many women hold back on their vision and sacrifice their goals to be "better" moms. Successful Mompreneurs use their vision to push forward in order to create a foundation of pride, success, and lessons of purpose for their children and other Mompreneurs-in-the-making.

What does having a vision mean? The dictionary definition of vision is "the ability to think about or plan the future with imagination or wisdom."[1] Author and leadership expert John Kotter describes vision in terms of something that helps clarify the direction in which to proceed. Like other experts, Kotter believes and has learned through his successful career that when a person knows what they want to accomplish, showing up daily and taking the needed actions to achieve that goal are much easier.[2] As working mothers, we also need a vision—a clear image of what we want our professional and personal lives to look like. When we create this vision, it will be easier for us to know what we need to accomplish daily so we can stay on our path to success.

Developing one's vision is not always easy. In their study on creating a vision that will lead to success in business, Jim Collins and Jerry Porras, co-authors of the business best seller *Built to Last*, note that fact. "A well-constructed vision comprises two elements, the core ideology and envisaged future. It takes time, focus, and courage."[3] In addition, your vision changes with time; just as we go through different chapters in life, our vision does the same and we need to adjust along with it.

When I was in my twenties, my vision was focused on making money. I was young, did not have a family, and had all the time in the world to devote to building my name in business; it was about making my mark and having my own "stuff." In my thirties the vision shifted; I was now a mom and also going through a divorce. I had a solid reputation in my career so my vision became about being a good mom, being able to live on my own, and showing people my strength. Now in my forties, my vision is focused on contribution and legacy: What messages can I share to impact others and how will I be remembered? All of these visions are fine. All of these visions are "correct" because they are true and mine.

As you create your vision, remember, there is no right or wrong way. This is about you and *your* vision—what is important to you.

Your vision is your passion, your belief, your driving force. It is what gets you excited and passionate to meet your goals and share your message. Your vision is your own—and you need to own it!

So how do you come up with your vision? Here are some tools to help you:

BUILD A LIFE LIST

One of the best ways to create your vision is to start identifying what you want your life to look like. Many people create a bucket list, or a life list—a list of items they want to accomplish to make their life fulfilling and have meaning. As busy women, we need to remember to live our lives, to enjoy moments and experiences. Life is not all about work and family, it is also about us; our lives matter too.

Sample Life List

Have	Do	Become	Give
Great relationships with my family and friends	Go on safari	A mentor	Time and funds to St. Jude Children's Research Hospital

When I do my life list, I have buckets for things I want to 1) Have, 2) Do, 3) Become, and 4) Give. These four areas are important to me and help to make my life full. Here are examples of each of my buckets:

- Things I want to Have: great relationships with my family and friends, a beach house, a best-selling book

- Things I want to Do: travel to places like Australia, go on safari, and skydive
- Things I want to Become: a *great* mom, a best-selling author, a keynote speaker, and a mentor
- Things I want to Give: create a foundation, donate time and funds to St. Jude's, and provide my son with an amazing life

Why is a life list so important? It gives us clarity and a path and direction for what we are working toward. My list reminds me of *why* I am doing what I am doing; it keeps me focused not on the hours that I put in, but on the impact I will make and what success will allow me to do in life.

When I teach, I have my students create their life list during their business planning. I like them to understand the real motivation for what they are doing. I want them to connect with why they need to show up daily and to create the excitement for the journey. Two people helped me to understand the importance behind creating a life list.

The first is famous anthropologist, explorer, and adventurer John Goddard, who began his list when he was a teenager. By the time he reached middle age, he had compiled a list of almost 180 items; additionally, he had completed a good third of them. Goddard understood that as you create a list it helps you become alive; you know what you are working toward and it allows you to make sure you live your life fully engaged. We do not have to be a world-famous explorer like John Goddard to appreciate the beauty and adventure of our own lives.

One of the things I notice when people make their list is that they get caught up in how they will accomplish items. They think of things they want and then their minds wander off to thoughts such as

"Wow, that is going to cost a lot of money" and "How will I be able to get away from work for that long?" or "That will never happen." Before they even write the item down, they have already given up, and the item they've dreamed of never even makes the list. Remember, the quality of your life is the quality of your list. *You* get to decide what you want your life to be filled with. You get to choose—design *your* life and dream a bit.

We get caught up in the *how* because we are fearful. We do not like to fail and we like things to be clear and certain. A life list is our dreams, and unfortunately, as we grow older, we tend to lose sight of our dreams coming true. This is where the second person to influence me in creating a life list comes in to play. He taught me about the vision behind the list.

During his early years in office, President John F. Kennedy stated that within a decade the United States would successfully put a man on the moon. This was a bold plan, but his cabinet was a little puzzled because, at that time, there was very little in place for the growth of the space program. Yet Kennedy knew that the vision came first, and the how would find a way. This has become one of my favorite ideas. We do not need to worry about *how* we will get something done *right now*; we just have to begin with the vision.

Our brains are amazing computers. As we enter data into them (in this case, the item in our vision), the brain then begins the process to find solutions to our problem; the brain is designed to make us right! As we focus on an item, say a trip to Italy, the brain will align us with items that show us how it can happen—maybe we would meet a person who just went, we may see an airline having a sale on flights, or we have a friend who also wants to go. The *how* begins to appear once we get clear on the vision.

Now, creating a list and just "believing it will happen" may sound weird and not very logical. It certainly did to me the first time I tried it. But it works! Here are some of the items I had on my list that I thought were (and still are) a little far-fetched:

- Writing a book: Within days, I started to meet and talk with people who had written a book, and I researched programs for self-publishing and ads on social media to help people write their first book. Eighteen months later, my first book was published.

- Going on safari: This is my dream vacation and will happen in the next few years. Every time I look at that item, I come across someone that is in the midst of planning a trip or has just returned. And they have valuable information that is helping me plan my trip.

The vision comes first. The *how* will find a way.

I encourage you to start your life list, and if you already have one, add to it. And after you build it, do not put it away; revisit it regularly. Keep those items fresh in your mind and let your brain lead you to them. Create the vision of the life you want, and the life you want will drive you, motivate you, and connect you with greatness. This vision will be your rocket fuel to keep you engaged and excited.

ASK WHY

Often our vision becomes our family's/kids'/company's vision, and we do not have a personal vision that is just for ourselves. The successful Mompreneur maintains a personal vision; she knows who she is, where she wants to go, and how to bring meaning and purpose to her life. As I mentioned earlier, having a vision helps you stay focused on your *why*. Your *why* is deep-rooted and has a lot of power in getting you to act and stay motivated. Your *why* is your inner passion and your true compass for what you are doing. Your *why* is your story, the thing you communicate by your words and your actions. It is what informs others of your truth and inspires them to follow and support you.

Most of us confuse *what* we do with *why* we do it. They are very different. *What* is the job. What do you do? I am an author, a speaker, a coach. *Why* is the meaning. I motivate and inspire others to greatness daily.

People have little response to *what* I do, but they get intrigued and excited to find out about the *why*.

Many times we see the *why* in a company's vision statement. It becomes the mantra, the lifeblood so that customers understand the company is about more than just employees showing up for a paycheck or for making a product. The *why* is the heartbeat of the company.

A good friend of mine had a shift in her *why* several years back. She was making an impact as a financial planner. She had many clients and was making good money. At the same time, she didn't have a strong *why*; she would show up, do her job, go home to her husband and baby, and repeat. Her life was fine but lacked meaning.

When her son was just a few months old, he was diagnosed with stage four neuroblastoma. Her world was rocked. In addition to connecting with the profound love for her child (who today is healthy, happy, and cancer-free), she learned three valuable lessons as a Mompreneur:

- We don't have forever. We have an unknown period of time to make an impact on our customers, clients, and community—on our family, relationships, and goals. We can't waste even a day.

- She was ready to think bigger. She made it through that difficult period and was able to produce just as much revenue that year as the previous years in her business, so she felt she had no excuse moving forward not to do extraordinary things while walking in a season without those adversities.

- What she does for her clients is life-changing. She determined that she no longer has just a job and isn't just a business owner. Instead, she has a *vision* for her business and considers her work as her calling.

These three items became part of her *why*. It was now not about financial planning but about helping her clients change their lives for the better. It wasn't about working more but rather smarter. And it was about *living* her life and not taking time for granted. As she got clear on her *why*, her business began to grow, and she has continually been recognized in the top ten producers nationwide for her company. She now has more balance and happiness than ever before.

People want to be a part of your *why*. When you are clear, others get clear too and they want to work with you. You attract the right clients who trust you and your process, and fit within your *why*.

Your *why* is your message. Make sure you know it and share it. The world is waiting to hear it.

CHECK YOUR ENERGY/DO YOU SMILE?

It has been said that you should do what you are passionate about and to some extent that is true. If you do not love what you do, the energy just will not be there. And others will feel that energy. Energy is transferred by what you feel and what you think, so if you do not really enjoy what you are doing or do not think highly of your job, people can tell.

I remember when I was younger and had a job as a telemarketer. I hated it. I didn't like calling to bother people, the product was not important (in my mind), and I was not doing anything impactful. It was no surprise that I dreaded going to work each day and could not make sales happen.

Today is so different. I *love* what I do. I look forward to my days and working with my clients. Please understand that I am human and there still are times that I do not want to work. Also, being that I travel extensively for work, I do not always love being away from my son, my dog, and my bed. Why do I do it? Because I love the impact I make; I love the people I meet and knowing that I can help them transform their lives and businesses. How can I not want to go and do my job? And you know what? My clients and students feel it. They can see my excitement and passion for what I do. They know I am not there to just get a paycheck and that also makes them more engaged with me.

You most likely do not love all aspects of *what* you do. It is again that *why* behind it. If you are working toward your *why* and your life list, the dots will become connected and everything will work together.

I have had jobs where I would cry on my way to work each day. Jobs where I wished I would get sick or hurt so I could get a day off, and ones where I lived in fear of being fired daily. That is no way to live. It will burn you out, disconnect you from your passions, and overall make you miserable.

Successful Mompreneurs flourish because they believe in what they do. They want to be role models and change the status quo in some way. They are not looking to simply make money but rather to make an impact. Yes, they are tired. Yes, they work hard, and yes, they love what they do, which is what keeps them going, even on the hard days.

Having a vision is the key to success. You need to understand and design a life that you are passionate about, both on the business and personal side. When you bring deeper meaning into your life, it stirs the passion inside of you; you know what you are working toward and you get excited. By having a clearer direction of what you want your life to look like, you become more passionate about how and whom you will connect with daily. It no longer is about scoring a sale, getting a new client, or simply working on a new project. It is about laying the foundation to achieve your life's vision. Make your mark and stand in your power.

You may not be there 100 percent today, but remember:

The vision comes first, the *how* will find a way.

ACTION STEPS

1. Work on your life list. Come up with at least five items in each of the following categories and start creating your vision:

   To Do   To Have

   _____   _____

   _____   _____

   _____   _____

   _____   _____

   _____   _____

To Become   To Give

_____   _____

_____   _____

_____   _____

_____   _____

_____   _____

2. Decide: What is your *why?*

_____

_____

_____

_____

_____

3. Biggest aha moment from this chapter:

_____

_____

_____

_____

_____

4

FACING AND OVERCOMING FEAR

Some women fear the fire.
Some women simply become it.

—R. H. SIN

Many years ago, I heard an interesting story that changed the way I looked at fear. A study was conducted that followed participants as they jumped out of a plane. What they found was that as the plane rose in elevation, the heart rates of the participants also began to elevate, but once they jumped out of the plane, their heart rates lowered. What this uncovered is that fear is not in the act; it is in the anticipation of the act. Or in simpler terms, we are not afraid of doing a specific thing; instead, the anticipation and thinking of the action make us fearful.

This really hit home with me. Many do not believe me when I tell them that I used to be afraid of public speaking. And when I say I was afraid, I was terrified! I would suffer anxiety and panic, lose sleep, and have paralyzing fear for days and sometimes weeks before a talk. However, once I started speaking, I was fine.

So, if we know that the *doing* is not where the fear lies, we need to have some tools to help us get through the *anticipation* of an act. Think about when you first had your baby. You were probably scared, unsure, and hesitant to do certain things. But you knew you had to—it was your job to make sure your baby was safe. Even though you experienced fear, you took action.

For me, I remember being scared to feed my son solid food for the first time. What if he choked? Would I know what to do? But not feeding him was not an option. Feeding him was something that needed to happen, which forced me to take action. Once I did, I realized everything would be fine. I was afraid of the what-ifs, but when I leaned in and took action, I noticed that the fear was not there.

We need to be able to build a bridge that will take us over or around the fear and get us to the side of accomplishment and success. For example, you may fear calling a client. Before the call, take a moment and think about the value you can bring to them with your services. Focus on that end result. Once you pick up the phone, you will be in action. The thing that stops you is the fear of not knowing what the client will say or the fear of possible rejection, but if you believe in what you are providing a client, it is much easier to take action.

Another example is asking for a sale or someone's business. Again, the fear of rejection can paralyze you and keep you from acting. To overcome this fear, you could rehearse the conversation prior to having it so you are more fluid in your delivery. Focus on truly knowing the value you are bringing to the table and prepare for possible objections that may arise so that you have your talking points together. When you are prepared, you will feel more confident, and when you feel more confident, you will be more likely to take action.

HOW TO BREAK THROUGH FEAR

Focus on your why

Why are you doing the thing you fear? Will it bring value to others? One of the best ways to get over your fear is to focus on *why* you are doing a specific act. What is the real purpose behind why you want to do this?

For me, I was afraid of speaking in front of large audiences. I was worried I would sound silly, look weird, and nobody would care what I had to say. I was focused on myself and not my *why*.

When I shared my fear with my mentor and dear friend, Larry Kendall, he asked me a simple question: "Do you believe the message you're sharing is important for your audience? Do they need to hear what you are saying?" My response was a resounding yes! I knew my message was powerful and could positively impact my listeners' lives. Larry taught me that it was not about what I was doing but *why* I was doing it. I needed to focus on the value I was providing instead of on myself.

You can apply this lesson to many aspects of your life. Let's go back to the example of jumping out of a plane. *Why* would you do that? Maybe it's to bring adventure into your life. Or it's a bonding experience between you and some friends. Or it could simply be that it's on your bucket list. The same teaching point applies: Do not focus on you but rather on the *why* behind the action. That will connect you with the action and give you the needed motivation to go forward.

As a Mompreneur, you need to do this too. Ask yourself some qualifying questions to help bring you clarity before you take action, such as:

Who are you helping?

If you do not provide your service/tool/product, how will that impact your client?

If you do not share this information with them, where will they get it? And will that be the best information for them?

If your client does not have you, how will they be able to move forward?

By not sharing and taking action, what value are you holding back from your clients?

For me, not standing up and speaking meant the audience would not have this valuable information. They would not learn about amazing tools and strategies to help them grow and achieve success. And if I did not share these things, I was letting them down. That is one of the reasons I wrote this book. I knew my story and experience could help other Mompreneurs. I felt alone and I do not want that for other working moms; I wanted them to have these tools and other helpful strategies so that it will be easier for them. And I knew if I did not write this book and speak on this topic, I would be letting my fellow Mompreneurs down and keeping them from success. That was not an option for me, and that is what pushes me daily to do things, even when it can be scary.

Get support—talk it out

It can be hard to see the other side when you are in the middle of things. A great way to get past the fear is to talk it out. When you can vocalize your feelings, you can often see opportunities you didn't think were there.

We've already discussed how difficult delegation is for Mompreneurs, and at the heart of that is a lot of fear. Hiring an assistant, for example, can cause a lot of fear and anxiety. Questions arise such as:

How do I find someone?

What do I pay them?

What do I *actually have them do?*

How will I find the time to train someone?

It can all be so overwhelming!

I know I had all of these feelings when I looked to hire my first (and subsequent) assistant. I chose to carve out time with my coach to talk it out. I asked how she and others she worked with made it work. I was able to see paths to success and create a plan that was tiered to make hiring an assistant more manageable and less fearful.

What does a tiered approach look like? It means breaking down your approach into smaller chunks and growing from there. Maybe you begin with an intern or a part-time assistant. Maybe you hire one person for a specific task. Many people are using virtual assistants or shared assistants. All of these options allow you to start the delegation process without having to fully commit to hiring someone full time. It also will permit you to try out individuals so you can find the best match for you and identify where you really need help.

Another fantastic way to get support is to hire a professional business coach. A coach will help you stay accountable to your goals and work with you to develop a plan that will enable you to take action. Over the years, not only have I been a coach, but I have also hired several myself. My coaches have helped me stay accountable, streamline my systems, and learn where I can push harder and when to pull back. One of the greatest benefits for me was that my coach helped me "stay in my lane" and not get distracted and stray from my goals and vision.

I tend to be an idea girl; I always have a new and exciting idea of what I want to create. That can be wonderful, but it also can overwhelm me and keep me from acting on any of my ideas. My coaches have helped me to make sure that the ideas I was following through on were in direct alignment with my goals.

So how do you find a coach? There are lots of ways.

1. Ask others. Many Mompreneurs are enlisting the help of a business coach and they will be happy to connect you if you ask.

2. Seek out a mentor. They may be willing to work with you at a higher level, or more likely, can refer you to a colleague who specializes in coaching.

3. Look online. The number of professional coaches has grown tremendously over the years. Conduct a search and you will find them.

If you do not have a coach, seek advice from others you know or admire. People are willing to share more than we give them credit for. You can join a networking group or even start one yourself. I belong to several online communities where I can ask questions, receive advice, and learn a great deal. If you prefer an in-person feel, organizations like the Chamber of Commerce and professional women's groups can be found in almost every city.

In addition, looking at the paths to success others have taken is a great way to create your own success. Look to others and talk with others. You might be surprised as to what tools and resources they can offer.

Consider the alternatives

When you face your fear, try to imagine the worst-case scenario. Then consider whether or not you can live with that outcome. What will happen if you don't face your fear or do something that might seem scary?

As I've discussed, one of the ways I help working moms is to connect them and share stories so that we all can learn and grow. This vision is wonderfully illustrated in my show, *The Working Woman's*

Channel, which launched in September 2021 and streams online (https://www.youtube.com/c/MomentsofClaraty/featured). In this show, I highlight working women and share real stories to success. It has allowed me to open my reach and ability to share information, tips, and inspiration to other women on a global level.

In season two of my show, I interviewed Carrie Nash. Carrie is a successful mortgage broker with more than twenty years in the business. After several (successful) years with the same company, Carrie decided to take a leap and move to a new company, one that many had not heard of before but one that could offer great service to her clients.

I asked her why she made the decision to move when everything was relatively fine where she was. Why would she decide to shake things up when it was not a necessity? Her answer impacted me. She said, "I looked at my life and the person I would be in ten years if I didn't make the move, and I didn't like what I saw."[1]

Even though everything had been going well at her company, Carrie needed to grow. She knew that if she let the new opportunity go by, she would become stagnant in her career, and all that she'd built would fall flat. It was not about the move, but about the alternative. She saw the alternative and didn't like it.

Sometimes we look at the alternative and it's more positive. If we push through the fear, the alternative may bring us a promotion, allow us to move to a new location, or start a new chapter.

Whether it is a positive or negative alternative, looking at the possible outcome can be motivating.

Build confidence and competence with practice

As professional women, we want to be confident in our abilities and the value our services provide. If we are not feeling completely clear on our value and goals, it is hard to feel confident, and therefore we do not always take action or secure business. When we are not confident, we hold back, may not ask the right questions, and could miss an important opportunity with a client. The best way to build confidence is to, first, outline our value and then, second, begin to practice articulating that value to others. This requires some role-playing.

Let's be honest, very few people enjoy practicing. It can be uncomfortable, and this act alone can cause fear. But it really works! When you are confident in your skills and know how to articulate your message, you can handle any situation. Practicing allows you to face potential objections ahead of time and workshop them so that when you are face-to-face (or on the phone), you will be ready for anything that comes your way and can handle any objections with grace, professionalism, and directness.

If practice makes perfect and will help us gain confidence and close more business, why are so many of us hesitant to do it? One reason is that we are afraid. This is because we are not clear in our skills, value propositions, and abilities. Practicing fixes that uncertainty! It allows us to get clear on our message and make sure we are delivering it with purpose.

Early on in my real estate career, I had to find and talk with prospective clients—you know, cold call. It was one of my least favorite things to do. I didn't know what to say, it was awkward, and I fumbled over the scripts. My boss required that all team members practice (role-play) daily for thirty minutes.

Yuck!

But we all did it, and you know what? It paid off big time! When calls came in, I was prepared. I knew exactly what to say and how to say it. It allowed me to control the conversations, have better connections, and create clients.

Think about it a different way. Before a surgeon conducts their first surgery on a real patient, who do they practice on? That's right: dead people! And we want them to do that. No one wants to be the first body that someone cuts into.

Doctors practice.

Attorneys practice.

Actors, athletes . . . everyone practices, and I bet they are afraid initially too. But they know they must practice if they want to become great at their craft. Because when you are good at your craft, you do not have to be afraid.

What are some things you should practice? Here are a few suggestions:

1. Saying *no*. If you must say no to something or someone, practice how to deliver this message in a few different situations so you can say no with confidence.

2. Holding firm on your fee. Knowing your value and what you bring to the table will allow you to respond fluidly and confidently about the cost of your services.

3. Asking for a difficult item or process. Knowing what to say and your reasoning before a conversation will make it easier to state your case.

The idea is that before you have a higher-level conversation, personal or professional, practice the dialogue and delivery before you work on the final product. Lee Cockerell, a retired executive vice president at Disney, wrote in his book *Creating Magic* to "never practice on your clients."[2] I think that is really good advice.

Even today I still practice. I practice dialogue with my coach, other instructors, and even peers. I still don't absolutely love it, but I do it because it makes me a better Mompreneur, and I no longer fear conversations because I am prepared and confident.

Breathe and do it anyway

Several years ago, Nike came out with its famous "Just Do It" slogan. And the company was right. Sometimes the only way through your fear is to simply take action.

Mel Robbins talks about this in her concept of the "5 Second Rule," in which she says that when you think about doing something, you have five seconds to take action otherwise the likelihood of your completing the task decreases.[3]

At times, action is the best remedy.

Remember our study on jumping out of the plane? Once the participants took the leap, the fear went away. I know I have experienced this many times in business and life. When I swim in the ocean, it starts off really cold. But after I swim for a bit, I become warm. In the same vein, when I am afraid to give a speech, I simply start talking, because I have practiced and am connected to my *why*. When I have to make calls, I just take a deep breath and dial.

While that initial fear may never go away (I still have fear before a talk), knowing how to face it and work through it are key. Identify what makes you afraid and use some of the strategies we've discussed in this chapter to face the fear head on.

You are stronger than your fear, and remember, fear lies in the anticipation not in the actual action. Get to the action, focus on the end results, and the fear will melt away.

ACTION STEPS

1. Write down something you are fearful of, personal or professional.

   _____

   _____

   _____

   _____

   _____

2. Describe the story you tell yourself about this fear.

   _____

   _____

   _____

   _____

   _____

3. Decide on one strategy you can use to face and move past the fear.

   _____

   _____

   _____

   _____

   _____

4. Who can help you move past the fear?

   _____

   _____

   _____

5. Biggest aha moment from this chapter:

_____

_____

_____

_____

_____

SECTION 2

SKILL SETS

Don't Strive for Fewer Problems,
Strive for Better Skills

5

LEVERAGING TIME

We think, mistakenly, that success is the result of the amount of time we put into work, instead of the quality of time we put in.

—ARIANNA HUFFINGTON

As busy Mompreneurs know, time is very valuable, and finding an extra moment in the day can be a challenge. We have demands from work, family, friends, and even ourselves. As we go into each day, we need to shift our thinking from simply how to manage our time to how to better leverage our time. When we manage our time, we look at what we are spending time on—calls, planning, clients, etc.—but when we leverage our time, we look not only at how we use our time but more important, if we are using time in the most effective way possible. We ask, "Is this the best use of this moment?" or "How can I get the maximum results from my energy?"

We all have the same amount of time, 168 hours a week, but when we can learn to leverage our time—to use it to its highest and best use—we can accomplish more. Note that accomplishing more does not mean *doing* more; it means learning how to do the right things.

One of the reasons we do not focus on our time is because we hold tightly to the concept of multitasking—the idea that we can do multiple things at one time. We think we can review reports while talking with clients, talk on the phone and work on a project, and write an email and attend a meeting, but the truth is that multitasking does not work.

Do you remember the fable of the fox that chased two rabbits? Well, in the end, he could not catch either one. He was multitasking. Like the fox, when we try to "chase" various things at once, we miss the real opportunities. Our brains are not wired to have us focus on multiple things at a time. Research tells us that what is actually occurring is our brain is switching rapidly between these multiple tasks, to the point where it appears simultaneous, but in reality, our brain is only able to handle one task at a time.[1]

Now you may be thinking to yourself: I have been multitasking for years and it's been fine, or even if I am not giving 100 percent focus to a task, I am still giving it attention and that is good enough. Yet, in telling yourself this, you are not taking into consideration the true cost of multitasking.

According to a recent study, when we multitask, it takes us three times longer to complete a task, and we do it with 50 percent greater error.[2] Can you imagine that? What if you told your clients that the project they hired you for is going to take longer and will probably have errors? Do you think they would hire you?

In his book *Time-Blocking*, author Luke Seavers talks about using the opposite of multitasking—single-focusing—as a way to successfully leverage your time. When you single-focus, you give 100 percent of your attention to one item at a time. This way, you are giving optimal attention to tasks so you can finish them in less time and with a higher degree of integrity and professionalism. He also notes that you can use single-focusing for both business and personal aspects.[3] The key to single-focusing is time blocking. This is the act of consciously making appointments on your calendar (for the day, the week, the month, etc.) for any recurring events or tasks as well as other important things you need to accomplish. When you block out time to focus on the right things, the right things get done.

So how do we leverage our time as productive Mompreneurs? Here are some strategies for putting together an effective schedule using time blocking:

PREPARE A WEEKLY PLAN

One of the best ways to leverage your time is to examine the time you'll have for the week before the week even starts. You want to both identify the time you'll have (and be honest!) and assess how you will use that time. You need to ascertain upcoming demands for the week and start determining where to put your focus.

I look at this like a business planning session. Remember, *you* are the CEO of your business and life. Any good CEO would take time to plan and map out the week before it began; they would meet with the different departments and teams to make sure all are on the same page. This is *your* company and you need to do the same, even if you happen to be in charge of all the departments.

The key is to keep it simple. Your weekly plan does not need to be complex. A good weekly planning session has three parts and takes approximately thirty minutes to complete. In the Appendix, I've provided a weekly success planner template you can start using now.

1. Reflect on your previous week

What happened? What went well? What didn't get accomplished? What were wins? How could it have been better?

I have my clients ask themselves these questions: *On a scale of 1 to 10, how would I rate last week? What could I have done differently to make it a 10?* This allows for reflection and growth. When we reflect, we learn. Keep in mind, you do not want to ask, "Did I get it all done?" You don't want to focus on "failure." Sometimes we did not get a task done because we needed to pivot and shift, so the focus should instead be "Did I get the right things done?" and "Did I give my best and do my best with the time I had in front of me?"

During this reflection, you don't want to simply check the boxes to make sure you "did it all," it is about looking at the week to determine *how* you showed up. You want to be honest with yourself and make sure you are showing up the right way, with the right energy, and focusing on the right actions on a consistent basis. There will be weeks where you got everything done, and others where you did not. As a Mompreneur, you want to be able to reflect and feel confident in what you *did* accomplish. Even if you didn't get all the items on your list done, make sure you gave it your best.

Some weeks when I reflect, I give myself only a 6; maybe I missed some targets or lost my energy midweek. Other times, I can give myself a 9 because I showed up each day and gave my all. The reason you should do this weekly is that you are looking for patterns and consistency; one week of missing the mark will not keep you from success, but several weeks in a row might. By reflecting weekly, you can look for patterns in how you are showing up and ascertain if adjustments or assistance are needed.

2. Identify the upcoming week's targets

Before you get your schedule together, identify the commitments you have already set. When you identify your targets, you are taking time to assess everything you need to address. You are looking at your targets for business, as well as any items in your personal life. During this time, you want to clearly lay out the following items:

- Who do you need to connect or follow up with?

- What important dates and deadlines are upcoming?

- What appointments are already set?

- What projects do you need to work on or complete?

- Any miscellaneous items that need to be addressed.

By examining your upcoming commitments, you can work to be more honest with yourself (and others) before you set your schedule.

One of my clients was being hard on herself because she was (in her mind) falling behind. When we looked at her schedule for the upcoming week, it became clear what the issue was. For this particular week, she had several personal and family commitments that left her with approximately sixteen hours, or two eight-hour workdays, to devote to business, instead of a full work week (forty hours). She was trying to cram forty hours of work commitments into those sixteen hours, which simply would not work. We needed to reset her expectations so they were more realistic and attainable.

As Mompreneurs, we must be honest with ourselves about the time we really have to dedicate to the upcoming week *before* it begins. This gives us a better chance of success and staying purposeful.

3. Put your schedule together

Once you are clear on your targets, you can put your schedule together. I know many of you may shy away from a schedule; you might want flexibility and freedom to run your business. But you still can have all of that. You need to change your mindset from seeing a schedule as constrictive and limiting to one that provides freedom and balance. Here's a great mantra to work on from leadership guru Michael Hyatt: "What gets scheduled gets done."[4]

Mompreneurs also know that there is a better way to do a schedule. Many businesspeople focus on scheduling only the work side; a Mompreneur doesn't do that—she starts with her life. After all, when you schedule time for your life, you get to have a life. Sound strange and difficult? It's not, so let's lay it out:

What works best for me is having my weekly planning session on Sunday evening. I block time as an appointment at 7:30 p.m., and I use this time (about forty-five minutes) to lay out all the preceding items. This little meeting has been so impactful in my life and business that I consider it one of my Secret Weapons (hint: You can find more Secret Weapons in the Appendix). The meeting allows me to see where my time and focus need to be for the week so I can work at my optimal level. Decide when your planning session should be each week and add it to your schedule. We'll delve deeper into putting a weekly plan together in chapter 11.

Successful Mompreneurs embrace time blocking. They view it not as a chore or even a habit, but rather as a tool and strategy to help them accomplish more in less time. When you clearly lay out your week and make time for your essentials (those core actions that will keep you in alignment with your vision), you can go into your week with the assurance and confidence that you will get the right items completed.

HAVE A GIVE-UP LIST

Here is the truth: You cannot do it all. Sorry, but that's the reality. And in truth, you should not want to do it all! A strong Mompreneur knows it is not about doing it all. Instead, as we've discussed, it is about doing the right things, the items that really need your focus and will be the needle movers for you in your life and business.

Now I know what you are saying: "Yes, I get it, but *how* do I make room for the right things?" One way is you use the three steps outlined previously to plan your schedule. The other is to create a give-up list. The idea is simple.

> ## To make time for the right things, you have to be willing to let go of the wrong things; you must make space in the time you have.

Think of it this way: When you were a child at the park, you played on the monkey bars. You had to reach for the next bar so you could move forward to the other side, but to move you also had to let go of the bar behind you. You must "give up" your grasp of one bar to propel forward. Life is not about staying still or in the same place; you must move forward, and to do that, you must let go.

Train your mind to know that time spent doing one thing is time spent not doing another. You need to not only leverage your time, but also free it up for the core foundational items in your life and business.

Here are some of the things on my give-up list:

- Watching television certain days of the week. I reinvest that time into reading/personal development.

- Staying up late. This way, I can be fresh and energized in the morning.

- Watching the news. This allows me to keep a positive mindset.

- Staying continuously connected to social media. Social media is an important part of my business, so I have allocated times to follow feeds and post. I am not giving up social media, just being connected to it 24/7.

We are not given more time, so we *must* make room in our current lives for the tasks that will guide us toward our goals.

Also, it is not all or nothing. You don't need to run this pattern every day. For me I focus on Sunday through Thursday, and I give myself a little clearance on the weekends. Find a pattern that works for you.

Think about where you spend the bulk of your time. Is it taking away from what you really need to do?

GET CLEAR: DELEGATE

As I've mentioned previously, you cannot do it all. Nor should you want to. A CEO knows that delegating is imperative for success, and it is also one of the things I see Mompreneurs struggle with most. In talking to and coaching Mompreneurs, I see three common themes that these women tell themselves:

- I can do this better.

- It will be easier for me to just do it; training someone will take more time.

- I am not worthy of having an assistant.

You must shift your mindset. The truth is that you *are* capable of doing these items, but you *should not* be doing them because they are not part of your daily role as the CEO of your organization or department. Your mindset should be that you are the CEO of your business, and any CEO has an assistant, if not more than one. A CEO is not weak because they delegate. Rather it is what makes them stronger and able to accomplish so much.

The first step in learning how and what to delegate is to get clear on your role as the CEO. When you look at the organizational structure of your company, determine what your purpose and active daily role is. Do you generate new business, market the business, share the vision, lead others? These are your Vital Few—the core foundational activities that are essential for you to do to ensure your success. Once you identify these key items, that is where you need to spend most of your time.

How do you know if something should be included in your Vital Few? Let me explain this by sharing a story.[5]

There was a professor teaching her class. In front of the room on a table she had six items:

- A large empty jar
- Five large rocks
- A pile of smaller rocks
- Some gravel
- Some sand
- A beaker of water

She began by placing the five large rocks into the empty jar and then asked the class, "Is the jar full?" Most of the students were not paying attention, so she continued and added some of the smaller rocks. The students could see where this was going and began to comment that the jar was not full. She continued with all the other items as they filled in the gaps and finally, as she poured in the water, they could all see there was no more room and that the jar was indeed full.

She then asked them another question: "What do you think would have happened if I had started backward and added the water first, ending with the larger rocks?" The students all agreed that if she had begun with the water, by the time the professor added the large rocks, the jar would have begun to overflow, therefore leaving no room for all of them.

The large rocks are the Vital Few. Most in business would say that items like meetings with clients are part of the Vital Few, and please do not misunderstand me, they are very important, but they are not one of the Vital Few. These meetings, in fact, are smaller rocks. Why? How do you get a client meeting? You can only create them when you do something else, like making calls or networking. Finding your Vital Few is an activity that moves your business forward. It is the catalyst to success and the keys to creating sustainability in your life and business. Your goal is to determine the large rocks that will become your Vital Few.

Let's look at an example. Julie is a top real estate broker in her market. She is very smart and capable of doing all the things required of a real estate professional: writing contracts, negotiation, marketing, holding open houses, et cetera. But not all of these are her main duties. Her core foundational activities—her Vital Few—revolve around generating new business. When I first started working with Julie, she was spending most of her time (about 80 percent) handling administrative duties. She would not be able to grow her business and increase her bottom line unless she moved away from the admin items and into her Vital Few.

Over the course of the next few months, Julie hired an assistant and worked to delegate the non–Vital Few tasks. As a result, in six months, her business grew more than 40 percent. By reinvesting that time into her Vital Few, she was able to increase her time spent in the Vital Few activities from 20 percent to almost 50 percent. With more time (and focus) devoted to her core activities, her business began to thrive. The small investment of a salary for her assistant made her almost three times the income.

Julie learned two key lessons all successful Mompreneurs must remember:

- You should not do it all.
- You should focus on your Vital Few.

I had to learn these lessons as well. Like many Mompreneurs, I was doing it all. In 2009, I was venturing away from my corporate job and moving toward being an independent contractor, so money was tight, and I needed to cut back on excessive spending. I was starting my business and knew I needed to invest to get it going, but I was also scared to spend the extra money.

I was a single mom with a young son (he was four at the time) and balancing grad school. Logically, I knew I needed help and someone to be there to offload my work demands on the administrative side, but I was also caught up in thoughts about not being worthy enough to have an assistant.

My fear led me to do everything myself—sales, admin, content creation, marketing, et cetera. As I focused on doing *everything*, I came to learn that I was not doing *anything* well. I was not an expert in many of these areas (especially marketing), so I was simply doing the basics and not the work that would have truly supported my goals. All my surface-level work spread across every area meant that I was not spending quality or focused time in the areas that truly mattered for me and my role in the organization (and yes, I call it an organization because regardless of employee size, I ran a business).

As the CEO of my company, I had to step away from the thought of what *can* I do to what *should* I do. Those are two very different things. I *can* do anything, but I needed to focus on what I *should* do—my Vital Few—including tasks such as prospecting and building relationships, creating content, and tackling coaching and training. As the CEO, that was my role. My role did not include filing, developing marketing, and other administrative tasks. Again, I could do these things, but I would never get my company to the level it needed to be if I was showing up as both a CEO and an administrative professional.

All of us Mompreneurs need to get clear on what we *should* be doing in our roles within our organizations. What are the Vital Few, or foundational activities, you truly need to focus on? These could include the following:

- Generating more business
- Putting together deals and negotiations
- Overseeing production
- Managing and coaching your team

You need to think about yourself as the CEO and determine what roles the CEO should perform daily. That is where your focus and time should primarily be spent.

When we get clear on our Vital Few and focus on those key activities, change and transformation in business and life happen. Even today, I work hard to make sure that most of my time is spent on my Vital Few: creating content, speaking, and networking. It does not mean that I never do items outside these Vital Few, but now my time is primarily spent on those activities.

Please note that I did not make this leap overnight. It was hard. I encourage you to take it slow and make regular progress. First, get clear on your Vital Few activities and the ones that are not vital. Begin prioritizing the tasks you can delegate and pick one area to start. Here are some ideas:

- Scheduling appointments. You can hire an intern or part-time assistant. There are also numerous applications you can use as well, such as Calendly.

- Hire a courier. This is someone that can drop off and deliver items to clients and other providers. This could be a case-by-case hire or someone you bring on part-time or as needed.

- Marketing. If you are not an expert in this area, maybe you hire a social media manager or someone to make sure your marketing goes out as scheduled.

- Lead generation. You can even hire people and companies to help you qualify leads to save you time,

In her book *168 Hours*, Laura Vanderkam discusses that as an entrepreneur (or Mompreneur) maybe the best place to start is on the home front, such as hiring a house cleaner or setting up automatic payments for bills.[6]

For me it was easiest to start at home. I began with hiring a house cleaner, while I had my son help with the laundry and other small tasks. This saved me between four and six hours a week that I could then reinvest back into my business or into my life (like taking a nap, for instance). Then I moved on to using a courier, a marketing assistant, and other items. I still probably do too much, but I am making progress.

You must remember that time spent doing one thing is time spent not doing another. Continue asking yourself if you are doing the right things for your role. How do you determine this? Go back to your vision—who is it you want to become? Focus on how that persona shows up in your day. For me, I want to be confident, purposeful, have strong connections with my people, and be in control of my time. The actions that I take daily need to support me in showing up as this person.

We will explore the Vital Few again in chapter 11, but to help you identify your Vital Few now, here are some questions you can ask yourself:

- What is my role in the company?
- What are tasks that I *must* do and cannot be handled by someone else?
- What brings me joy? What do I like to do?
- If my role requires a license/certification, what tasks require work to be done by someone with a license versus without?
- What tasks, if not done, will hurt the growth of the business?
- What are my clients/customers expecting from *me*?

TAKE TIME OFF

As successful Mompreneurs, we cannot be our best if we are tired, burned out, or sick. Time off allows us to reenergize, refocus, and pivot. To serve others, we must take care of ourselves. Taking vacations is great, but remember to take time during each week as well. I take at least a fifteen-minute walk outside between coaching calls; I take naps midday to give me energy and my brain time to rest; and I take one weekend a month off the grid so I can rest and get centered.

Find what works for you, but time off is crucial to your success.

Time is valuable. So many of us try to do more, when we really need to do less at a higher level. Work on leveraging your time to increase productivity and focus. In the next chapter, we'll talk about the importance of self-care and how to make time for it.

So, my Mompreneurs, what do you think? Are you looking at time differently? Keep up your mantra:

It is not about doing everything but doing the right things.

Always remember, you are the CEO of your business, and you have earned the right to have others help you.

ACTION STEPS

1. What day is best for you to do your weekly planning session?

_____

2. List your Vital Few or core foundational activities:

Business   Personal Life

_____   _____

_____   _____

_____   _____

_____   _____

_____   _____

3. Choose the items that must be on your give-up list:

_____

_____

_____

_____

_____

4. List three things you can delegate:

Item: Who Can Help You:

_____   _____

_____   _____

_____   _____

5. Biggest aha moment from this chapter:

_____

_____

_____

_____

_____

6

THE NECESSITY OF SELF-CARE

Life is not measured by the number of breaths we take,
but by the moments that take our breath away.

—VICKI CORONA

I remember when my son was about three. I was starting my business, getting my master's degree, and still working at my "real" job. Oh, and I was a single mom too. I was exhausted, and I could tell I was starting to crack. I knew something needed to change, but what? I had no time to do anything more. I was running on empty, but I knew if something didn't change quickly, I would have a complete breakdown.

Lucky for me, my mentor (who was also my previous boss and a good friend) saw the breakdown coming and insisted that I start taking care of myself. She had been in leadership for many years and was no stranger to observing how people push themselves past their limits and begin to break down, causing not only issues in their job, but also huge health ramifications. Knowing that I was a classic overachiever, she knew I was headed in that direction and wanted to help interrupt the pattern before it led to a breakdown. I sort of laughed . . . *Yeah right, let me just take a weekend off and go to a spa, right?*

Take a day off. How was that going to happen? I know you have wondered the same thing. How, with work, family, and more, can we possibly entertain the idea of taking time off for ourselves? In some strange way, as women, we feel the idea of taking time for ourselves is selfish. It is a luxury that we just do not have time for. The flip side to this is that self-care *is not* selfish; it is necessary and one of the key ingredients to success and sustainability.

My mentor also reminded me that if you are on an airplane and things go bad, you need to put on *your* oxygen mask first before you assist others with theirs—even your kids. The idea is simple: You cannot adequately help others unless you take care of yourself first.

As Mompreneurs, we spend a great deal of time and effort looking after others, but who is looking out for us? If we do not stand up for ourselves, our well-being, and need for care, no one else will (this is not a dig at our significant others . . . it is just how it is). We *must* be ambassadors for ourselves. As such, we must make sure we take care of ourselves and get the rest and nutrition needed to perform at our best levels. Proper self-care allows us to have the energy needed to face all our responsibilities and whatever tasks are ahead of us that we'll need to take on. Just like the ambassador of a country, we are here to advocate for and protect ourselves so we can truly show up for others.

I mentioned that self-care is not selfish. In fact, self-care may be one of the most self*less* things we can do. Self-care allows us to indirectly help others even more; when we take care of ourselves, we can better take care of others. The feeling that self-care is selfish may be real, but it is backward and will start to work against us and our goals.

We need self-care and "playtime" for optimal focus and effort. In fact, if you pay attention to most successful people, they all say the same thing: We need to take care of ourselves. For example, in her *New York Times* bestseller *The Sleep Revolution*, Arianna Huffington writes: "Disconnecting from our technology to reconnect with ourselves is absolutely essential for wisdom."[1]

Another story we often tell ourselves as Mompreneurs is that if we are not available to others, if we are spending time on ourselves, then we will be letting others down—meaning our clients and family. But the truth is this: If you show up as anything less than the best version of you, are you really taking care of your clients and relationships? Self-care is what allows you to be there for your people in the way that they need you. You will deliver a higher level of service, which will allow you to gain trust and strengthen relationships. Taking care of *you* is taking care of others, and taking care of others is what builds relationships, trust, and successful businesses.

In business, we learn to take care of our greatest asset, which in most cases we believe is the client, but we are wrong. Our *greatest* asset is ourselves. If we do not take care of ourselves, the rest of the company (regardless of whether you are a company of one or one thousand and one) will suffer. As a Mompreneur, you must shift your mindset and believe in the truth: *To best serve your clients and your family, you must make time for self-care.*

We are no good to others if we are burned out, sick, or rundown. If we want to perform at our optimal levels and give the best that we can each day, we must take care of ourselves.

I want you to stop for a moment and go back to being a kid. When you were stressed out and had pent-up energy and frustration, what did your parents tell you to do? Mine would tell me to get out of the house and go play. Playtime was a necessity, not just to keep my parents from strangling me, but also for myself; they knew that playtime brought comfort and joy and relieved stress.

As adults, we don't play anymore.

When we are playful, we have fun. When we are having fun, we experience less stress, frustration, and fear. Yet even though I know we Mompreneurs need playtime, I was left with the question of *how* we can find time to fit it into our already demanding schedules. With the many obligations we have as busy Mompreneurs, how can we find the time to take care of ourselves? Here are some tips to help you incorporate self-care into your life so you can show up in all areas—work and personal life—energized, focused, and ready to deliver your best.

PLAN IT

We must schedule time for self-care. It may sound silly, but it is true. As you learned in chapter 5, the things that get scheduled get done. As basic as this concept is, we need to carve out the time. As a coach, I encourage my clients, when filling out their weekly calendar, to schedule their self-care first. Most people do this backward; they first schedule all their work demands, then their family commitments, and if there is any time left over (which there rarely is), they might find time for self-care.

I plan my week differently. The first thing that goes on my calendar is my self-care. I block out time on my schedule for my workouts, downtime, fun, et cetera—and these times are *appointments*. I do this not only for myself, but also because my people need me to do this. I *must* take care of myself to best show up for them: my clients, my associates, my family, and my friends. After this time is blocked, I go to family obligations, and then I block time for work. Please understand that this is my planned week; it does get altered, but that is if, and only if, it makes good business sense. I am in control and make the decisions on what to adjust.

I know many people (and this could be you) who simply do not believe this type of schedule is feasible—but it is. Here's the key: You *must* make self-care a priority. We make time for the things that are important to us. I get asked all the time, "How do you make the time?" The answer? "I just do!" I know self-care is a priority and necessity for me to achieve my goals; it is less about working out and more about being able to show up with my peak performance level.

So what keeps us from planning time for self-care? I think it can be a couple things. First, we see it as frivolous. We buy into the story that only unsuccessful people can take time off or that downtime is reserved for the ultrarich who have the time for free time. Second, we worry that if we are not available for a client or a family need, we will let someone down and possibly lose their trust (and maybe business). Lastly, if we cannot give our all to it, we just won't do any of it; if we cannot find an hour for a task, anything less is a waste of time, and then we, as busy Mompreneurs, tend to simply drop the whole idea.

When you plan for self-care, I want you to keep in mind that this is about *progress not perfection*. You do not have to be perfect, such as working out every day or planning hours of "me time" each week. Mompreneurs can get overwhelmed in the planning and scheduling of time for self-care; they think it requires large blocks of time, but it does not. Doing something is better than doing nothing, and even a short ten- to twenty-minute effort will pay off when done consistently. Here are some ideas for quick self-care that you can do in under fifteen minutes:

- Meditation. Even just two minutes gives your brain time to rest and clear.

- Walk around the block. Get moving and allow fresh air to clear the mind.
- Laugh. Watch something funny on TV, YouTube, or another medium.
- Plank position. Maybe do three sets and hold for thirty to sixty seconds.
- Stretching. It's a great way to start the day.
- Journal about positive things. Relive the good times and discover the beauty in each day.
- Squat jumps. They are my nemesis, but I do ten a day.

I suggest you start small and work into the new habit. Carve out smaller blocks of time between business or family appointments for your self-care appointments. I often will block fifteen minutes between my coaching calls and use that time to stand up, stretch, take a walk, or even snuggle with my dog. Even two minutes a day of simply turning off the noise around you can be a wonderful respite. As you do more self-care, you will 1) find renewed energy and focus and 2) realize that you *can* step away from business for a little bit and the world will not come crumbling down.

SHARE IT

We cannot keep things a secret; we need others to get involved and help us. When we share our goals and intentions, it brings in accountability. Once you have a plan, tell your family, your friends, and your coach, and ask them to help you focus on your goals and give encouragement.

I am working hard on losing a little weight and getting leaner.

Part of this is because I want to look good (nothing wrong with that, right?), but more importantly, I *need* energy and health to do what I do. I cannot teach for eight or ten hours a day if I am tired and my body hurts, it's hard to run and catch a flight if I am out of breath, and my brain is not as sharp as it needs to be for my coaching if I am not feeding my body with better nutrients. So getting healthier is just as much about serving my clients as it is about serving myself.

I really thought I could do it all on my own, after all I am a coach, right? Oh, was I wrong! I began making excuses, would only put in half the effort, and get bored. With food, I would sneak too many snacks and not buy enough of the good stuff to keep me healthy. Not only was I gaining weight (almost twenty-five pounds!), but I also had little energy, was often light-headed, and not getting proper nutrition. I needed help.

I saw a friend of mine on Facebook who had lost weight and was looking fierce, so I asked her what she was doing (expecting I could just copy her process). In talking with her and learning that the key ingredient to her success was having a trainer, I knew I needed to follow suit. By sharing my goal with others, I now have a trainer that knows exactly what I want to accomplish, stays close to me to keep me accountable, and creates a plan I can follow.

In addition to sharing my goals and getting help from my trainer, I get help from my family and son. I have asked them all to support me, not to tempt me with snacks, and to ask me how I am doing. I know they are looking out for me, and I want to make them proud. Often, my son even works out with me!

Now, your goals for self-care may not be around fitness and food; maybe they're around taking time off, going on vacation and *not* taking your business with you, or simply doing more with those you care about. Regardless of how you want to bring in self-care, you need to share that goal with others around you so they can support you and help you with these targets. As Stephen J. Bronner points out, "A 2015 study published by the American Psychological Association said that people are more likely to achieve their goals when they closely monitor their progress, and the chances of success are boosted if progress is publicly reported or physically recorded."[2]

BE ACCOUNTABLE

Sharing our goals goes hand in hand with being accountable. Whereas sharing allows us to include others in what we're trying to do, accountability is the follow-through to ensure you get a specific task done or reach a larger goal. Accountability is the yucky part because it requires discipline.

The fact is that discipline is not easy or fun. Having a partner to keep you accountable makes it better. This is one of the reasons my coaching clients have a strong result in their businesses and lives—they are paying to be held accountable. You see, it is not about knowing what to do—we all know that—it is following through on an action that matters, and having an accountability partner helps with the execution.

This was an area of struggle for me. I have lots of ideas, but I struggle with follow-through and execution. A couple years ago, I was not meeting my goals; I had plenty of ideas and a ton of energy, but I was all talk and little action. My accountability partner, another strong woman with more than thirty years in her field, finally called me out. She said, "You know, I love all your ideas but are you actually going to do anything? Because I'm tired of just hearing about them." *Wow.* Those were strong words but exactly what I needed to hear. It was her job as my partner to push me and hold my feet to the fire. Within a few weeks, I had new clients, my first book written, and several other projects near completion.

Being held accountable can be scary and hugely uncomfortable, but it works. And it works in all areas of our lives, for professional and personal goals. Mompreneurs have accountability partners for a wide range of items that include making business calls, waking up earlier, working out, and even booking time for vacations. As humans, we want connection, and we want to know we matter. An accountability partner gives us this. We have someone to connect with who is looking out for us and pushing us because they know we can accomplish great things. Here are some tips to keep in mind when looking for an accountability partner:

- Do not use your best friend. You can get too comfortable and not give your best effort.

- Focus on specific areas of growth. It could be a project, growth in number of clients, or a skill set.

- Set regular meetings. I meet with my accountability partner every week for fifteen minutes, and we cover the following questions:

  ◦ What happened in the last week?

  ◦ What are my goals/targets for this week?

  ◦ What do I need help with?

Tell your accountability partner how to push you; they will need guidance for what works and doesn't work to motivate you. Be honest as well. This is a relationship based on trust, so you must be open and honest to get real results. Finally, success is not an accident. When I lacked accountability on reaching my goals, I wasn't going anywhere, but once I had a partner to push me to take the actions needed to reach those goals, success followed.

BE HONEST

While it's important to be open and honest with your accountability partner, you also need to be honest with yourself. At the end of the day, if you say you are going to do something, you must do it. I encourage you to be honest about what you *will* do and have the time to do, not just what you *think* you should do. If you are not excited about the task, you will be less likely to follow through with it.

I am not a runner. I ran track in high school but as a sprinter. As I was working to get in shape, I noticed that everyone having success was running, so I was convinced if I ran, I would get in shape too. But again, I am *not* a distance runner. I don't like it; I don't want to do it. So, every night as I went to bed, I had a little conversation with myself. "OK, when we go out for our walk tomorrow, let's add in some running." The morning would come, and I would not run. I repeated this conversation with myself for months. Finally, one day I just said to myself, "Look, Self, you are not going to do it. You will *never* want to run, so stop saying you will. Just walk and do something else you will enjoy. You don't *have* to run." And that was the end of the debate. I gave myself permission to not do what I thought I *should* do and decided to do what I wanted to do and *would* do. Now I walk, do yoga, online HIIT (high-intensity interval training) classes, and barre. More importantly, I do what I say I am going to do. By choosing to do things I enjoy, I am more excited to show up and do them *and* to keep doing them; I no longer make excuses or avoid the activities but instead look forward to completing them.

So, as you get ready for your days, look at your schedule and determine what self-care goal is realistic for *you*. Maybe it is something like these:

- A simple fifteen-minute walk outside
- Working out from home to eliminate the need to drive to a gym
- Reading rather than watching the television
- Listening to a podcast instead of music in the car

Decide what is best for you and what you will enjoy. You do not have to do what everyone else is doing; focus on what brings *you* both joy and results.

And just as we want to be honest about the activity, we also need to be honest about the time commitment. Some days you may have an hour, while other days you may only have five minutes. Practice this mantra:

You do not have to do everything, but every day, do something.

It is better to be consistent with small actions than to be marginal with others; it will be better for you in the long term to do a daily ten-minute workout than to do only a single hour-long workout a week.

GO TO SLEEP

I think I would be missing a huge point if I didn't use this time to discuss the importance of sleep to self-care and performance. One of the biggest mistakes I see working women make is that they compromise their sleep. They give so much to others and the demands around them, that they cut back on one of the most critical parts of self-care, which is proper sleep.

So why do we do this? Well, simply put, we have a lot to do, and we tell ourselves that we will be able to catch up on sleep over the weekend, on vacation, or sometime in the near future. The reality is we never do. Until we shift our mindset around sleep, we may never change this dynamic.

I was the same way—up at 4:30 a.m., in the office by 7:00 a.m., work, work, work, then go home to work more until around 10:00 p.m. My body was tired, my brain was tired, my emotions were spent. But I kept going.

Then I read Arianna Huffington's book *The Sleep Revolution*, and I finally began to understand the power and necessity of good (and regular) sleep.[3] Sleep was not something to be taken for granted or to be ignored. Nor was it something frivolous. Sleep, in truth, is the most important factor in living a healthy, full, and productive life. Good sleep is the key in determining success.

To illustrate this point, let's dive a little deeper. Inadequate sleep comes at a price. The total annual financial cost for poor sleep in Australia in 2016–2017 was $17.9 billion, of which 68 percent consisted of productivity losses largely due to absenteeism.[4]

Lack of sleep also leads to poor memory-related processes. Sleep deprivation impairs memory and learning, compromising the benefits of these training efforts. Sleep deprivation also undermines efficiency in switching among tasks, increasing task-switching costs and compromising performance.[5]

Mompreneurs know that a lack of sleep correlates to a drop in customer and client satisfaction.[6] When you are tired, you may not show up fully present. I know my clients could see my exhaustion in my face and also in how I showed up. I was not as "bubbly," my concentration was off, and I forgot items and would repeat myself. If your customer or client is wondering if you are firing on all cylinders, they may lack confidence in your ability to be their best option.

And if you still don't see the importance of getting proper sleep, inadequate sleep is associated with a myriad of chronic health conditions, including cardiovascular diseases (e.g., stroke, hypertension, myocardial infarction), diabetes, and psychiatric disorders including depression, substance dependence, and suicidal thoughts and behaviors.[7]

Too many women compromise sleep. They do not see that good sleep is not only needed, but also imperative if they want to deliver quality service and personal experiences and raise trust with their business partners. On top of that, without sleep we jeopardize our health; if we lose our health, we will not be able to show up for anything or serve anyone.

For me, sleep is critical to my productivity. I am a person who needs a solid seven to eight hours a night. I know many can work on less, and some need more. I have learned what I need and I make sleep a priority. So much so, that all of my friends know that I shut down at about 8:00 p.m. If I am at a party, dinner, or simply just hanging out, when the clock hits eight, I am outta there! It has become a running joke in my close circle, but that is OK. I need to do what is best for *me* and I do not feel guilty about that.

But it was not always this way. There were times I would push myself to stay up to work, socialize, whatever, and then I would struggle to wake up, I would be tired the next day and would not have great focus. My suggestion regarding sleep is to make it a priority and start small. Here are some tips I have used over the years:

- Go to bed thirty minutes earlier. It is not a huge difference but starts to add up.

- Take a nap. My sweet spot is forty-five minutes, but many state the benefits can be seen with just twenty-five minutes.[8]

- Sleep in one day on the weekend or at least sleep until the body wakes up without the use of an alarm clock.

- Every three months, disconnect for a day or two. Give yourself and your brain a break.

My challenge for you is this: Every day do *something* for self-care. Even if only for a few minutes. You do not have to always give your all, just be honest about what you *will* do—and do that. A little bit of something is always better than a lot of nothing.

You need to take care of yourself. Not only will you benefit from it, but those around you will too. I am a better coach, trainer, writer, friend, and mom because I take care of *me* first. Self-care allows me to show up daily as the best version of myself and focus on and connect to those I interact with. Take care of yourself. Others need you strong, healthy, and full.

ACTION STEPS

1. List some ideas for quick self-care that you can do in under fifteen minutes:

_____

_____

_____

_____

_____

2. List some people you can share with and who can hold you accountable:

_____

_____

_____

_____

_____

3. Biggest aha moment from this chapter:

_____

_____

_____

_____

_____

7

COMMUNICATING LIKE A MOMPRENEUR

Speak your mind, even if your voice shakes.

—MAGGIE KUHN

We all know that quality communication is the center of success. Connecting with others and getting on the same page are critical parts of growth and sustainability in business. As Mompreneurs, we have an even higher need for quality communication. We are busy; we juggle business, after-school events, doctor appointments, deadlines at work, cookies for bake sales, and veterinary appointments—if we are not clear and on top of our communication, balls will be dropped and things will fall apart. We need to ensure our communication works, not just in business with our peers and clients, but also on the home front. Our families and clients are counting on us. They need us to communicate with them so there is no confusion and things run as smoothly as possible.

There is a difference between basic communication and *quality* communication. Quality communication allows us not only to connect with others, but also to ensure they understand us. As Mompreneurs, we want to make sure we are not simply sharing our thoughts, but also allowing for empathy, understanding, and (hopefully) agreement. In short, we have to communicate like a mom boss!

To assure quality communication, which will lead you to successfully attain your goals, you want to look at a few different areas:

1. How to position yourself to be understood and reach agreement with the party you are communicating with

2. How to communicate your goals and vision

3. How to use communication to establish boundaries and standards

COMMUNICATE FOR UNDERSTANDING: THE PLATINUM RULE

One of the biggest reasons we don't achieve understanding through our communication is that we are talking to talk and not positioning our communication for understanding. In my Ninja Selling classes, we teach the concept of the Platinum Rule. What's the Platinum Rule?

Do unto others as they would like done to themselves.

Now you might be thinking, "Oh, I know that one," but chances are you are more familiar with the Golden Rule, which is a little different: Do unto others as you would like done unto yourself.

Let's lay that out again:

Treat others as *they* would like to be treated (Platinum Rule) versus treat others as *you* would like to be treated (Golden Rule).

You see, the latter is focused on *you* and *your* needs, and the former highlights the party you are communicating with—*the other person.* Just as platinum is stronger than gold, considering others when communicating is more effective than only considering yourself. We know that quality communication is contingent on the other party understanding us, so being able to communicate in a manner that connects with the other person is going to be more successful. By utilizing the Platinum Rule, you are not talking in your language but rather in *their* language.

How do we do that? Well, effective quality communication *is* a skill set and it does take practice, but it is also pretty easy to learn, and the results can change the game.

One of the easiest ways to look at and understand this concept is through identifying personality traits people use in their communication. You can use key identifying markers to adjust your words, tone, and delivery to connect better, which will result in a higher quality of understanding.

To illustrate this point, let's look at one of the most recognized personality assessments—DiSC.

UNDERSTAND YOURSELF AND OTHERS BETTER

DiSC identifies four different personality profiles: Dominance, Influence, Steadiness, and Conscientiousness.[1] For my purposes, I prefer the terms *Driver, Influencer, Supporter, and Controller.* Here are some of the identifiable traits for each profile:

- Driver: future-oriented; quick decision-making; focus on strategy and outcome; seeks risk

- Influencer: present-oriented; quick decision-making/ impulsive; focus on fun and enjoyment; seeks risk

- Supporter: past-oriented; slower decision-making; focus on trust; avoids risk; more reserved

- Controller: past-oriented; slower decision-making; focus on statistics, trends, and gathering information to ensure they will not make mistakes; avoids risk

These are basic descriptions, so if you want to go deeper into the personalities, see My Favorite Things in the Appendix for a list of websites, books, and certifications you can explore.

So, what do these profiles mean in relation to the Platinum Rule versus the Golden Rule? *Everything.*

Picture for a moment that you are a real estate professional and you are a Driver personality. You are meeting your client for the first time.

You: "Hi. I have our day lined up and we are going to see three properties today. The market is moving fast so you're probably going to have to make a decision today and pay full price." How do you think your client may respond? Well, if they are like you, a Driver—ready for quick decision-making and someone who embraces risk—you will probably be fine. But if your client is a Supporter or Controller, you could turn them off, shut them down, and lose the client completely.

Let's try this scenario again using the Platinum Rule:

You: "Hi, it is so nice to meet you. We're going to see some great homes today. In this market, properties are moving pretty fast and also going for full price in most instances. I've prepared a packet to help give you all the information you need. I don't want you to feel

rushed or pressured, and know you can trust me as your advisor."
By focusing on what they need—calling out key words such as *trust*
and *not pressured*—you can connect on a deeper level with the client.
When you speak their "language," the client will feel more comfortable working with you and internally believe that you can help them.

The Platinum Rule is designed to connect you with the other
party. The truth is that people prefer to work with others that are like
them. So, what are some things you can look for and pay attention to
in trying to determine someone's personality to better connect with
them? Look for: What are the words they use? Are they more extro-
verted or introverted? Are they more vocal or are they quiet? Here's
where the DiSC profiles come into play. Review the list of traits. Do
your client's actions or words fit one of those categories more than
the others?

Once you have an idea of your client's personality, use communication strategies that best work with that personality, while always keeping
the Platinum Rule top of mind. For each profile, do the following:

- Driver: Use bullet points, get to the point quickly, and focus
  on the strategies you will use to help them achieve their goal.

- Influencer: Keep it fun and fast-paced. Engage them and
  include them in the process.

- Supporter: Slow down and work to gain trust. Demonstrate
  how your process will make it safe and take care of them.

- Controller: Give them lots of information so they can look at
  all angles.

This process doesn't just work in business; it will also work in your
personal relationships. For example, if you want your kids to clean
their room, you can position your request in their style:

- Driver. "Clean your room so you can go play." Or tie the request to an allowance.

- Influencer. "Let's make a game out of this." Or have a reward system.

- Supporter. "I trust that you will finish cleaning your room, and when you have a clean room, you can find all the things you need and not lose anything."

- Controller. "Everything has a place. Let's create a system: You can make your bed first, then organize your closet, et cetera."

Another tip in effective communication is to prepare for your conversations *before* they happen. Before I enter into a discussion that requires higher-level thinking and decision-making, I follow three steps:

1. What is my objective for this conversation?

2. What is it I really want to say?

3. How can I frame it in the other person's language, using the Platinum Rule?

Let's see how it works using an example with my son. Say I want him to clean his room. How can I accomplish this in the most effective way possible? I need to consider the following:

1. **What is the objective?** To get him to clean his room *now*.

2. What **do I really want to say?** You are driving me crazy, and if you do not clean your room *now*, we are going to have a major issue.

3. **How can I frame this request to communicate it best?** It depends on my son's personality profile. Here are some things I could say based on each one:

   - Driver: "I have left getting your room cleaned up to you and clearly that strategy is not working. What is a different way we can approach this and get this done?"

   - Influencer: "We need to get this room cleaned. Maybe we can do it together, or after you clean it, I'll have lunch ready for you."

   - Supporter: "We really need to get this room cleaned. I know it's boring and not fun, but trust me, once it's done, you'll feel better and be able to find everything you need."

   - Controller: "Do you know the level of germs and bugs that are attracted to your room right now?" Or "I think you're making a mistake by not cleaning your room."

When we communicate using the Platinum Rule, we establish

- Better understanding
- More empathy
- Greater end results

It takes a little time, but it will allow you to build better and deeper relationships long-term. Your people will appreciate you, and you will be able to reach your desired results much faster.

COMMUNICATING YOUR VISION

Why is it so important to communicate your vision? Buy-in.

We need those closest to us to understand *why* we are doing what we are doing and *how* it is going to affect them. We cannot achieve our goals and dreams without the support and buy-in of those closest to us. When they become aware of our purpose and plan, and also how they are a part of that plan, they will be more encouraged to help us achieve success.

To help you gain support, there are two concepts to understand:

- What's in it for me?

- What's expected of me?

Quality communication needs guidelines and expectations. These two concepts help with that. When you clearly set forth how your vision will bring you closer to your goals as well as benefit others, then your clients or your team or your family will be more inclined to step up and support you in making those goals happen.

When I began traveling for work, it was challenging. My son was still younger and many people questioned my motives. They felt I was just chasing the money and not taking my role as a parent seriously. I knew that was not the case, and I also realized that the only way others would understand my true purpose was if I did a better job of communicating it to them. Rather than simply stating what I was doing, I took the time and effort to explain *why* I was taking this action and how achieving my goals would benefit them as well.

So that is what I did. I sat with my ex-husband, his wife, and my son, and together we talked about my job. I explained what I was teaching and how it was going to positively impact my students. I went over how, when I was growing my business, I felt lost and alone, and how I did not want that for others, especially other working moms.

I was able to convey that what I was doing was not just a passion for me, but also an obligation—I had a message that was going to unlock others and allow them to avoid the mistakes I did on my path. I shared the purpose of my classes and how they impacted the participants, and even showed them some of the comments from the people who attended my classes. By clearly articulating the impact my role had on changing others' lives, I made it clear to the people in *my* life that my career was not a matter of simply "making money," but was focused on improving others' lives.

In addition, we talked about what all of us needed to do to make my goals happen. We went over a calendar, how we would communicate while I was on the road, and how I needed to be more present when I was home to make up for the time I was away. Some of the solutions we came up with included helping my son with homework over FaceTime, sending cards to my son so he received something from me when I was away, and planning special quality time together for when I was home.

By taking time to communicate how my goals also could help them reach their goals and how we could all work together, hitting our objectives became easier. It is not always perfect, but it certainly has helped.

As Mompreneurs, it is important we share our voices. We all have something important to say. Our goals, our lives, and our messages matter. When we tell others our story and allow them to see how it connects back to a larger vision, not only will those who support us get it, they will want to be a part of our vision too. Communicating about our goals allows others to join us on our Mompreneur path. And as Marianne Williamson wrote in *A Return to Love*, "as we let our own light shine, we unconsciously give other people permission to do the same."[2]

As you lay out your goals, think about those around you who can become a part of achieving your vision with you. Determine how your wins can also be their wins and how all of you can work together as a team. For example, if you must work long hours, you can set aside a date night or time for family dinners. Or if you must travel, schedule designated times to call and talk with each other. When there are deadlines, plan something special to do together after the deadline happens.

The more you talk—*really* talk—the better understanding you will have. Do not assume others around you, even those closest to you, understand your vision. Share it with them. Allow your family, friends, significant others, and partners to become part of your vision so they know you have and are continuing to achieve success with them in mind. The more you bring those close to you into your vision and show them that you cannot do it without their support, those you love will know you have considered their feelings in making your decisions. In return, not only will those around you be more support- ive, but they will also become your raving fans!

BOUNDARIES

As you share your vision and your supporters' part in helping you be successful, keep in mind that you need to establish boundaries as well. A boundary is simply a way to show a limit to an area, where there is an end point or a place one can and cannot go. Boundaries are not bad or negative; they allow for focus and growth. Boundaries also need to be communicated. As Mompreneurs, if we do not clearly define what is and is not allowed, others will not know our limits and therefore will not respect them.

Most boundaries come in the form of time management, and we

have discussed many of those strategies in an earlier chapter. As you use those strategies, be aware that you must be able to communicate your boundaries.

For example, if I am going to work and need focused time, I want to let my family, team, staff, and clients know that I am unavailable during those hours. This is what I call "bubble time"—a tight bubble of time I use to focus on activities without interruptions. Now that my son is older, I can share my schedule with him; he knows when my first appointments are each day, when I have breaks, and when I am free to be there if he needs me.

The importance of having boundaries around my time was a lesson I learned several years into my career. Before then, I was working long hours, approximately 4:30 a.m. to 10:00 p.m., taking every call as it came in, and was basically tethered to my job. I had no life and was completely burned out. In the talk I gave on Season 3 of Amazon Prime's Speak UP episode, "Burnout/Breakdown/Breakthrough," I shared the story of how I fantasized about getting into a car accident just so I could get a few days off to rest and not be bothered. How tragic is that? I didn't need (or want!) the accident, of course. What I needed were boundaries.

My mentor taught me the power of simply not giving in and not giving up my time. She taught me one simple phrase: "I would love to help you at that time; however, I have a previously set appointment. I am available at this time . . ." I was astounded at how that simple sentence worked! Most people easily accommodated my schedule, which allowed me to better control my time and my life.

The biggest hurdle in setting boundaries is fear; we are afraid to push back. Often this shows up as working moms being "people pleasers," that woman who wants to say yes to everything and everyone. She does not want to miss an opportunity.

Why do women do this? According to life coach Dr. Saloni Singh, people-pleasing is common nature for a lot of people, regardless of their gender. "People believe 'I'm not good enough.' That's something they don't what people to know because they want others to like them. There's a lack of self-acceptance, self-love. That's when they start exhibiting people-pleasing behavior," she says.[3]

I want you to repeat after me: When you try to do everything, you end up doing nothing. When you try to please everyone, you please no one.

You simply cannot do everything. It's just not possible. If you say yes to everything or have no boundaries, pretty soon your time will not be your own and you will be running on empty. At that point you will find that you also cannot show up to do the work that really matters and spend time with those that are truly important to you. Boundaries give you this freedom; boundaries allow you to show up for the right things and for the right people.

So how can we set boundaries?

Schedule

The best place is to start looking over your schedule to see where you need to be and the commitments, in both life and business, that you have. From this you can be honest about your time and what you can give. From here you need to block time for those important items and share your schedule. One thing I have learned is that when I share my schedule and let those around me know when I am available and then *I truly show up* for the times I promised, they can be flexible with me during the other times. For example, if I promise to be home for dinner and I make that happen, they can forgive me for being ten minutes late on another day. Show up for the promised commitments.

Rely on resources

Have resources to help you. You do not have to be a superhero and have all the answers. Make sure you have a list of others who can help when you are not available. This could be an assistant, a partner, or even someone else who can provide the needed service. When I sold real estate, the clients mostly called me directly, but they also knew that if I was not available, they could reach out to my assistant or even the service providers, like the lender, if they needed to. We all worked as a team; they knew the others I worked with were qualified and had access to the information to help them.

Keep promises

Follow through on promises. If you are unavailable, let others you work with know when you will be available to meet and talk, and then actually show up during that time. If you have a voice message that states you will return calls before the end of the day—do it. If you tell a client you need to research an item and you will call them back in a couple of hours—make sure you do. Your people will wait, but they need to trust that you will follow through on your promises.

I know the need for and importance of being there for my clients, but at the same time, if I am with another client, I cannot simply stop what I am doing to answer an email or message; that would not be professional. I tell my clients that my goal is to connect back with them within a three-hour window. That way they know my commitment, and we have an agreement. It is my responsibility to adhere to that promise.

I understand that having good communication can be easier said than done, but we must try. The more that we lay out guidelines, ask for what we need, and set the stage for expectations, the easier it is for all to move forward. Those who care about us want us to be success-ful, and sometimes we just have to explain the importance of a task or commitment and the significant role our people play in helping us achieve our goals.

ACTION STEPS

1. Name someone you need to have better communi-cation with:

   _____

   _____

2. By using the Platinum Rule, decide how can you share your goals with them. Use the questions "What's in it for me?" and "What's expected of me?"

   _____

   _____

   _____

   _____

   _____

3. List one boundary you can set in your business:

   _____

   _____

   _____

   _____

   _____

4. Biggest aha moment from this chapter:

_____

_____

_____

_____

_____

8

THE ART OF NO

An honest no is always better than a dishonest yes.

—CHRISTY WRIGHT

OK, Mompreneurs, buckle up! This is one of the most important chapters and also one that will be challenging for many of you. But if you can trust in me as your guide, this skill set can become your greatest ally.

Here is the simple truth: You cannot do it all.

We are all busy and the demands of life are growing each day. It is nearly impossible to keep up. Especially when it comes to running a successful business and keeping sanity on the home front. So, what do we do?

One of the greatest secrets to success is in learning how to say no. Steve Jobs once said that he was just as proud of what he didn't do as he was of all that he did accomplish.

I know that many of you as you read this have already started with the self-talk and the fear. So for a moment just let this message sink in: *You cannot do it all.*

As a coach and speaker, I work with people on this reality all day long. It is one area where Mompreneurs really struggle. I learned the power of the word *no* when I hit a wall; I was overworked and tired and did not have time for the important things in my life. I had sold myself on the idea that doing more would create a vision that I was successful, people could count on me, and I was important. But by saying yes to everything, I found I could not do anything very well. I would make simple errors with spelling, run late, appear disheveled to my clients, and on some occasions, even miss deadlines.

All of this led me to become burned out, unhealthy, and almost fired from my job. And I think my family was ready to fire me too. I was so focused on being there for everyone else that I was not there for me. And it all started to crumble.

I had to learn to say no. There was no other option.

A key thought to remember: When you say yes to something, you have to say no to something else.

As busy Mompreneurs, we are pulled in many different directions each day. With never-ending demands from family, coworkers, friends, and our job, it can be hard to know what we should do and what we should pass on. Plus, we want to be there for others; we like to help. But again, if we spend all our time and energy helping others achieve their goals, when will we have time for our goals, both professional and personal?

THE POWER OF SAYING NO

In saying no, we want to make sure we are not coming from a place of negativity, but rather one of focus and productivity. We need to start looking at our time as an investment and knowing that when we choose to do one thing, we are also choosing to not do another. Basically, before we say yes to something, we have to make sure we are not saying no to something more important to our business and lives. So, how do we determine what we need to say no to?

One strategy that has helped me is to first get clear on what I am saying yes to, so I can understand what I need to say no to. When an opportunity arises, I ask two questions:

1. Does doing this make good business sense?
2. If I agree to do this, what will I have to say no to?

These two simple questions will bring you insight and clarity in making decisions. If the opportunity does not help me or support my business goals, or if what I need to give up doing doesn't work for me, I say no. End of story.

Here is an example. I was invited to speak at an event in another state. When I picked up the phone and heard the offer, my initial response was "YES, I CAN COME." But before I committed, I went to my two questions. In looking at the opportunity, I realized the location for the event was not going to be easy to get to; it would take me a full day of travel there and back, taking me away from other clients, as well as obligations I had with my son. In addition, the group I would be speaking to was not my target audience, so I would not be bringing them as much value, and they were not people I would bring on as personal clients. So in the end, this opportunity was not going to move me toward my long-term goals, and it did not make good business sense at the time. That's why I said no.

Yes, I missed out on a paycheck, but I was able to work more with my current clients, be there with my son and dog, and use my time in my home office to work on business development, which would bring me more clients . . . and the right clients.

Remember, you cannot do it all. You must choose. So, make sure that when you make a choice, it is in alignment with your goals and does not take you off focus from what is most important in your life and business.

CHOOSE YOUR BRAIN TRUST

It can be hard to make decisions on our own. So many ideas sound great. You may need others to help you decide what you can and should say no to. I call this support group my Brain Trust. If I have an idea or an opportunity and have difficulty deciding whether I should go forward or pass, I go to my Brain Trust. This group is my center and keeps me focused. They ask me questions and help me look at the opportunity from all angles. Sometimes they just laugh and shake their heads at me because we all know the right answer.

Members of this group can include people from any area of your world. They can be mentors, coaches, coworkers, partners, or friends. However, choose the people in your Brain Trust carefully. They can be your best friend or significant other, but they don't have to be. The key is to look for people who are honest and not afraid to be honest with you and who are clear on your goals. You want to choose people who can help you and protect you from making poor decisions that can affect your business and productivity and keep you from living your true vision.

You want them to push you as well. And when they push, you know they come from a place of love. It is important to have those close to you push you; it is easy for us to hold back or to play small. Allowing them to challenge you will put you in a position to truly grow and experience more of what you need to achieve your goals. Go into these relationships knowing and expecting that they will challenge you, so you must have faith in them that all they are doing is meant to help you stay on your path.

Trust me, it is not always easy to hear this feedback, but it is necessary. Again, this is why I say choose the people in your Brain Trust carefully and trust that they are sharing feedback to support you and not hurt you. Recently, I launched a new TV show, *Living Real TV*. My business partner and I went through many possible titles for the show. We had one that we thought was great and perfect, but the Brain Trust disagreed. At first I felt sad and a little deflated, but the points they made truly made sense and allowed us to develop an even better title. If you ask for feedback, you have to be willing to listen. By trusting in your group, it will be easier to be open and receptive to new ideas.

BE REAL ABOUT WHAT YOU CAN AND CANNOT DO

There is only so much time in the day. We each get the same amount—168 hours a week. So you need to be honest, not only about what you want to do, but also what you need to do. Determine what the highest and best use of your time is. And only do those things.

In her podcast, *The Christy Wright Show*, business owner and speaker Christy Wright has said: "An honest no is always better than a dishonest yes." You must be honest with people.

Many wonder if women have a harder time saying no versus men. Even though there is no study that specifically determines this, many who study this phenomenon claim that most men are raised with the notion that saying no is acceptable, whereas women are taught to be more polite and accommodating. Based on how women are raised (in most cases) we fear saying no. We worry we will hurt feelings, lose business, or miss out on something. So we agree to do things that really are not in our best interest and then we build resentment and resistance. We must learn to understand that saying no is OK and give ourselves permission to say no.

A few months ago, I was putting together my Brain Trust (some call it a mastermind group) and invited one of my good friends and a successful businesswoman to join. Her response:

"I am sorry, but I need to decline. I just do not feel I can commit to this at this time." My response: "Great answer!" She was honest with me, and I would rather have her tell me no than to commit and not participate when she was there.

So learn to be honest about what you can do. Others will appreciate your honesty, and it may even empower them to do the same in their world.

IDENTIFY THE RIGHT CLIENTS AND COLLEAGUES

You must trust that the right people will support you. Live in abundance, not scarcity, and the right people will come to you.

I often see people lose control of their time because they give it to the wrong people. Far too often we take on the wrong client, employee, or vendor who is not in alignment with us, and it never goes well. We run in circles, build frustration, and often lose sight of the things we really need to do.

This has been a hard lesson for me to learn, and quite honestly, I still make this mistake. And it costs me every time! When I step outside of my system and decide to work with someone who is not the right fit for me, I lose time, focus, and energy. I remember early on as I built my coaching business, a potential new client wanted me to make time for them at hours that were outside of what I wanted. But I didn't have a strong client list and this person was willing to hire me and pay me! So I said yes, and it quickly went downhill. Due to the time difference, it was late in the day for me and I was tired. By this time of day, my young son was home and needed me. And did I mention I was tired??? I could not show up and give my best to this client, and they felt that too. I should not have taken her on as a client because I knew I would not be able to show up the way I needed to. Lesson learned.

Here is the reality: You do not need to work with everyone. You need to identify the people who will respect you and your process. Just as we evaluate our time to see if it makes good business sense, the same is true for the people we work with and spend our time with. We need to ask: "Does working with this person make good business sense?"

One of the strategies we use in the Ninja Selling program is $E = MC^2$. When we teach our students (most of whom are in real estate) to focus on choosing the right clients, we tell them that the Expectation to serve the client and help them achieve their goals needs to equal the client's Motivation, Communication, and Cooperation. How this lays out is that if in listening to their client's goals and expectations, the motivation to buy or sell is missing, and if they will not agree to quality communication or they will not follow the process, we encourage the agent to pass on the opportunity.

If we work with the wrong clients, we waste time, energy, and money. We cannot meet the expectations, and generally, the transaction goes poorly. It is not about the client being good or bad, it is about what is *best* for them, for you, and your business model. You need to give yourself permission to walk away when necessary and not feel guilty.

How do you know if someone is a good fit?

This can take time and patience. For me, it was a lot of trial and error (lots of error), but in time, I learned to look for signs and better vet my people. Here are some tips to help you learn how to identify the people you want to work with, whether clients, employees, or vendors:

1. Be very clear on your process and system. As you explain how you work or the results they can expect, the right people will be excited to work with you and follow your system.

2. Ask really good questions and *listen*. They may be interviewing you, but you are also interviewing them. Take time to gather the needed information to uncover their motivation, expectations, and goals. If you do not believe you can help them reach those goals or deliver on expectations, be honest and walk away.

3. Pay attention to whether you like them or not. Let's face it: Life is too short to work with jerks. If you do not like them, get a bad feeling from them, or simply do not enjoy their company, it is OK for you to pass on working with them.

EXPLAIN WHAT YOU CAN DO

Most of us have a need to help and connect, and we want to honor that. In saying no, our focus goes to a place of negativity. We see saying no as a disservice to others. One strategy to combat those feelings is to focus on what we can do instead of what we can't do.

For example, you may not be able to do the exact thing they are asking for help with, but you may be able to do something else. Here are some ideas on how you can respond:

- "Maybe I can meet with you at a different time?"
- "Although I'm unable to help you now, I'm happy to refer you to someone else."
- "May I give you some tips to help you locate the information you need?"

You can still be of service to them even if you do not do it yourself. Successful Mompreneurs know that saying no is one of the best things they can do for themselves. It will put you in control of your time, your business, and your life by giving you a system to make sure you are only doing the things that support you, your goals, and the vision you have for your life. Others will always ask you for things they want, but that doesn't mean you have to stop what you are doing to focus on their needs. Remember, you can still serve them even when you say no.

ACTION STEPS

1. What is one thing you struggle saying no to?

_____

_____

_____

   a. How is this affecting your ability to be more productive?

_____

_____

_____

b. What strategy from the chapter can you implement?

_____

_____

_____

2. Who are three people you need in your Brain Trust?

_____

_____

_____

3. What is your aha moment from this chapter?

_____

_____

_____

_____

_____

SECTION 3

ACTION GOALS
Without Action, Goals Are Just Dreams

9

CREATING HABITS THAT STICK

I am what I am today because of
the choices I made yesterday.

—STEPHEN COVEY

uccess is not an accident—it is a choice. Choosing to be successful comes from the habits we develop and then use daily. It's easy to talk about establishing great habits, like getting up early or managing our time, but why do so few Mompreneurs succeed at creating them? If we know that creating and keeping good habits are the keys to long-term success, why do so many of us struggle—and even more of us fail—to keep them?

Before we discuss strategies to create and maintain habits, let's first define what a habit is. A habit is a learned automatic response with specific features.[1] So habits are actions that we teach ourselves to get a desired result. We establish a set of rules for a specific action to get us from one point to another, based on the result we want.

Habits are found everywhere in our lives from making coffee to showering and even driving the car.

Habits are all about repetition; they are the little things we do over and over again, often without even thinking about it. They just happen. Our lives are full of such repetition. In fact, one study had participants record what they were thinking, feeling, and doing on an hourly basis. What the researchers found is that an estimated 43 percent of the participants' actions were performed almost regularly and usually in the same context.[2] Furthermore, particular actions, such as eating different types of food, tend to be performed in particular physical locations. What this suggests is that habits are automatic, and most people do the actions without even thinking about their performance.[3]

Habits can be both good and bad, of course. Everything is a choice; so too are the habits we create. If you want to be healthy, you may develop a habit of drinking water throughout the day. But if you also have a habit of keeping chocolate in your desk or having a caramel macchiato every morning, you may be undermining your effort to be healthy.

One reason we have difficulty establishing good habits is because we do not have a structure in place that will support and sustain us in doing so. Another reason is that we create habits that are unrealistic, designed by someone else, or that we don't feel connected to, and therefore we have no motivation to follow through over the long term.

To create a good habit, you first need to identify the behavior you want to modify or the particular outcome you want to achieve. Then you determine which actions will form the right habit that will support your desired result.

A purposeful and determined Mompreneur understands the power of good habits. This doesn't mean she loves them—after all, habits are not always fun, but she knows the importance of having good habits in achieving her goals. So what are some good habits for Mompreneurs? Here are a few to consider developing (or you might already be doing these!):

- Use mornings to get organized for the day. Good habit: Set aside ten minutes the night before to lay out and review tomorrow's schedule.

- Use drive time to listen to something motivational for personal development. Good habit: Before the week starts, key up one or two podcasts or audiobooks and have them ready and available.

- Make lists to be more efficient. Good habit: Write down who you need to connect with during the week and their contact information, so you have that ready to go when you make your calls.

- Create and follow a schedule. Good habit: Set an appointment with yourself to plan your week before it starts.

What habits would you like to set or have tried to set, whether for your personal or business life? Think about what barriers you put in place to keep yourself from doing so. How do you break through those barriers so you can establish great habits and make them stick? Let's look at four suggestions that can help.

1. GET CLEAR ON YOUR *WHY*

We discussed having a purpose, or *why*, earlier in the book. Your *why* is your rocket fuel for your actions and dreams. It connects you to them and gets you passionate about moving forward. Having a clear vision of your *why* is imperative to keeping good habits.

In his best-selling book *Atomic Habits*, James Clear states that the most effective way to change your habits is to focus not on what you want to achieve, but on who you wish to become.[4] Therefore, successful habits are rooted in the vision we have for our lives, personally and professionally.

Being clear on your vision will give you the motivation to push through and practice new habits, even on the days you don't feel like it. Most people, however, lack clarity about the one thing that really drives them, the one thing that will push them further than they have been pushed before. As a Mompreneur, what drives you to keep going, even when you feel like giving up? It is important to be clear on your *why* and how to use that as fuel to move forward and perform your habits daily.

Your vision also serves as a compass. Everything you do as a Mompreneur relates back to your *why*—your actions, who you choose to work with, your schedule. It all goes back to your vision of who you need to become. Keep your vision close and let it guide you through your days.

Is there a connection between motivation and habits? Absolutely. In my opinion, keeping good habits is all about our motivation, or why we are doing something. When we know why we are doing a certain action or working toward a particular goal, habits are easier to create and follow. An article in *Positive Psychology* magazine states, "Motivation is a vital resource that allows us to adapt, function productively, and maintain wellbeing in the face of a constantly changing stream of opportunities and threats."[5]

Another study showed that without motivation, our drive can diminish and we are more likely to give up.[6]

Let's look at some examples from my clients to see how a person's motivation helps them follow through with keeping habits. The *why* for one of my clients is giving back to her community. She set a goal to raise $10,000 for organizations near and dear to her. So she uses photos of the people she will be donating to as her motivation to keep her committed to her habit of making sales and connection calls with her clients. This is something she will procrastinate on or even avoid. Now, every time she wants to stray from her sales calls or goof off, she looks at those photos and remembers why she is doing what she is doing. This allows her to stay disciplined.

Another client wanted to buy her dream home. When she looked at the cost of the home and broke it down, it really was only a few hundred dollars a month more than her current mortgage. She knew that the work effort necessary to make the extra money was attainable. This is what kept her motivated. Every time she considered not following through or giving up on her habits, like making her daily client calls or getting into the office early, she thought of her dream home. It was this vision that allowed her to stick with her habits, and in under a year she was home sweet home.

My motivation is all about impact—helping others unleash their greatness. This is what drives me. And I don't want to help just a few Mompreneurs; I want to help *all* of them. It is my connection to this vision that feeds my soul and gives me the fire to show up daily. I have set up disciplines and habits to help me stay consistent. When I feel low energy and want to sleep in, I have the habit of looking at my schedule for that day and who I will be connecting with. Knowing who I get to help that day gets me out of bed. When I write, I visualize who will be reading my work and this helps me stay creative. Focusing on the women who will read my stories and grow from them is what gets me to my desk. When I want to be lazy and not work when I have not met my goals, my habit is to revisit my goals and the person I want to become. I know that putting in the one extra hour can transform another's life. It is this vision that helps me to deliver my best every day and not give up. Each day I have an opportunity to serve, to help, and to allow another Mompreneur to live her dream—this is what keeps me in my habits.

Knowing our motivation ties to our ability to not only form, but keep, habits. As the *Positive Psychology* article notes, the benefits of motivation are visible in how we live our lives. As we constantly respond to changes in our daily lives, motivation helps us to take the necessary action to deal with those fluctuating circumstances.

2. HAVE A SYSTEM AND MAKE IT EASY TO USE

When things are easy to do, we do them. When you are creating a new habit, identify the steps needed to do it, and build an easy system to help keep you in check. For example, if your desired habit is to watch less TV and read more, the first step might be to remove the batteries from your remote and put them in another room where they are not easily accessible. Second, you could place a book on your coffee table. This way when you go to sit down, the easy thing will be to read and not watch television.

I want to drink more water, so I always have a filled water bottle on my desk and on my nightstand. Grab, drink, repeat. The habit continues.

You can also build an easy system around working out. Lay out your workout clothes and shoes the night before so you can grab them easily in the morning. Put your gym bag in the car so it is always there.

From a business standpoint, if you need to have crucial conversations with a client or employee, you could practice the dialogue with a peer before you have the conversation, or even take time to outline the objectives, key points, and delivery method. This is something I have done and still do. Before I reach out to a client, I ask three questions:

1. What is the objective of this conversation?

2. What really needs to be said?

3. How can I frame and deliver it so they truly hear the message?

By going through these three steps, I get clear on not only what I want to say, but how it needs to be delivered. Once I have it all laid out, I can then rehearse it with a peer if needed. Many times, I use my weekly business planning session that I do before the week starts to identify the conversations I know I will be having. Other times it happens on the fly, so I just give myself a moment to regroup and prepare.

The easier it is for you to follow through on an action, the more likely you are to not only do the activity but also stick with it. You don't have to create a system from scratch to help establish habits. Remember the weekly planning session we discussed in chapter 5? Not only is this a great habit to form in and of itself, but you can also use it to help stay on top of habit-forming actions. I go into more detail on how to build your weekly plan in chapter 11 or you can jump to the Appendix for the template if you want to get started now.

Another solution is to use a contact relationship management (CRM) system, which can help you not only house all your contacts and their information, but also set up reminders, automatic drip systems for mailing and emails, reports, and more. There are hundreds of CRMs to choose from, and based on your industry there is probably one that will be a perfect fit for you.

3. CREATE AN ENVIRONMENT TO FOSTER AND SOLIDIFY YOUR HABIT

We become products of our environment. In writing about mastery for Ninja Selling, author Stewart Emery notes that you need to remove anything around you that promotes your being "average." As you work to develop (and keep) strong habits, make sure your environment is set up for excellence. A successful Mompreneur knows that she becomes a product of where she spends her time. Is your current house/office/car/etc. set up for your success?

If you want to eat healthier, stock the refrigerator with healthy food and put away junk food so it's difficult to get to—or just don't buy it! This is a challenging one for me because I *love* bad food. I know it is not good for me, but as it sits in the pantry, it calls to me. I have had to come up with some creative options to help me resist the "voices." Not buying the food was not an option for me: My son enjoys his cookies and treats, and he is a kid and I feel he deserves to have them (with moderation). Self-control when it comes to junk food is not my strong suit, so here are some things I do to help me maintain a healthier eating habit:

- I put my son in charge. He both cheered me on and policed me. If I went for the bad food, he would call me out. This built a little game with us and it included him in my success.

- As he got older, I tied it to cold, hard cash; if he helped me be successful in not eating chips and cookies, he was rewarded.

- I created a separate cabinet for junk food/snacks. That way I just would not even open the cabinet and see them. Outta sight, outta mind.

These might sound childish, but they worked for me. Although I have a lot of motivation when it comes to my work life, when it comes to sweets and treats . . .

You can also establish a good environment in the business realm, whether you work from home or in an office setting. For example, one of my clients wanted to focus on her sales calls so she created an environment where it was easy to do this. It started with the design of her office; she painted it yellow—a bright and cheerful color to get her excited and one that made her feel happy. She also added a comfortable chair and brought her office equipment—computer, scanner, and copier—up-to-date. She now works to keep her office clean and free of clutter. This "design for success" motivates her to come to the space daily and make her sales and customer calls. After creating a pleasing and highly functioning office, she turned her attention to setting up a customer database that is easy to run and access. All of this makes it easier for her to show up and be successful.

For many Mompreneurs, their second office is their car. Here are some things you can do to design your own on-the-go environment: Keep your car clean so that the clutter doesn't bog you down and clog your brain power. Have adapters and power cords in the car so you can stay connected (but remember, don't text and drive!). When I travel, I always have my battery pack so if my phone dies, I can pull over if driving or plug in at a coffee shop and be back in business.

As mentioned previously in this chapter, another option is to use drive time to listen to audiobooks or podcasts. Keep a favorites list and have the episodes downloaded before you get into the car so they are easily accessible.

4. GET A BUDDY AND MAKE IT FUN

Accountability works. As we discussed in chapter 6, when you have someone checking in on you and helping you stay the course, you show up. It is easy to feel alone and like you are battling this world and all the demands on your own, but you are not alone. For

Mompreneurs, it is important to have one or more persons you can check in with and partner with along the way. A buddy can be there to not only check in on you and your progress, but also be there as a support system when you start to feel overwhelmed.

Still wondering if you need a buddy? Well think about this: *Performance improves* when people know they are being held accountable by others for their actions; they work harder. Research shows that when someone publicly shares their goals, they have around a 65 percent chance of success. However, having a specific accountability partner boosts that chance to 95 percent.[7]

As a coach, my job is to help people stay accountable. But in your world, this could simply be a friend who is willing to help. When I wanted to start waking up at 5:00 a.m., I got a partner. She was another Mompreneur I met through networking. Together, we checked in via text each morning. We started at 6:45, then 6:30, then 6:15, until we both reached the 5:00 a.m. goal. Getting up became about the two of us succeeding, not just me.

Look around and see if there is someone in your circle who wants to accomplish a similar (or perhaps even a different) habit, and work together.

Several of my clients are in real estate so they need to make a lot of phone calls. To make it easier and more fun they do it in groups. They pick a time and all go to the office where they make calls together. Afterward they join up for lunch or happy hour. They find that the habit is easier to keep when they do it together, and then who doesn't want to go out and celebrate their good discipline, right?

I had another client that wanted to be healthier by simply drinking more water; she was a big soda and coffee drinker and knew that water would be a better option throughout the day. So she did two things. The first was using an app she put on her phone to track her water intake. She also asked her friends and family to support and encourage her. At home, they would only let her drink water with lunch and dinner. If she went out, her friends made sure she didn't order soda. After about a month, she was feeling better, and it was easy for her to let go of the soda and coffee.

These examples may seem simplistic, and they are! That is the point—keeping your habits can be simple. Like most things, we tend to overcomplicate them. Yes, you can hire people to help you, but you also can use resources that are right in front of you and *free*.

We are stronger when we work together.

Remember, success is not an accident; it is a choice. As a Mompreneur, you need to ask yourself if you are ready to make the choice to succeed. Ask yourself if the habits you have today are aligned with your dreams for tomorrow. If they aren't, take steps now to create those habits, keep them, and set your course for a successful future.

ACTION STEPS

1. Pick one habit you want to create over the next thirty days:

_____

_____

2. Connect this habit to your *why*:

_____

_____

_____

_____

_____

3. Outline the steps you need to take to create this habit and make it stick:

_____

_____

_____

_____

_____

4. Decide how you can improve your environment to enable you to create and keep your habit:

_____

_____

_____

_____

_____

5. Describe how you can make your habit fun:

_____

_____

_____

_____

_____

6. Name who will hold you accountable:

_____

_____

_____

7. Biggest aha moment from this chapter:

_____

_____

_____

_____

_____

10

CREATING YOUR
ENVIRONMENT AND CIRCLE

Surround yourself only with people
who are going to take you higher.

—OPRAH WINFREY

We are a product of our environment, good or bad. As a Mompreneur, you need to surround yourself in an environment that not only supports your success, but also cultivates the needed energy and focus that will drive you to produce amazing results.

The environment you build includes both the physical space as well as the people and messages you engage with. If you want to ensure success at the highest level, you need to make certain that all items in that environment are focused on positivity, performance, and greatness. This chapter demonstrates how to survey your environment—both the physical space and the people you surround yourself with—and make the necessary changes that will enable you to thrive and succeed.

YOUR ENVIRONMENT

Where do you spend most of your time? Where do you get most of your work done? Is that space set up for success?

When I began working from home, I needed to create a home office. We had a sunny, spacious second bedroom, but at the time, my son was young, and I wanted him to be close to me. So I gave him the cheery bedroom next to mine and decided to finish my basement and create an office in that area instead. I painted the basement a bright yellow, brought in furniture, and hung motivational photos. I knew I needed to keep the area open and bright to help feed my success. *But* at the end of the day, it was still a basement. There was only one window, which didn't allow in natural light. It was cold (and living in Colorado, the winters were *reallllly* cold). It simply felt like a basement versus an office I was proud of.

When my son turned thirteen, I made a change. He moved into the basement and created his "man cave," and I moved my office into his old room. It was on the second floor with vaulted ceilings, a large window, and a ton of light. I painted it, moved my furniture in, and now I *love* my home office.

What's the point of all this? You need to enjoy where you work. Your space needs to be a place that will spark creativity, encourage you to produce your *best* work, and get you excited to be there. If you do not like going to your place of work (whether a home office or an office building), that gray cloud of energy will follow you there daily.

How can you create an optimal workspace? Here are some tips:

Paint

Do you have a favorite color? Something that motivates and inspires you? Color can create emotion, which leads to energy.

In addition, there is science that backs how the right (or wrong) color can impact productivity and motivation. A University of Texas study found that bland gray, beige, and white offices generated feelings of sadness and depression, especially in women, while men experienced similar feelings in purple and orange workspaces.[1]

Here are some other factors to consider if you are thinking of changing up your office color. Blues and greens have a calming effect and help to improve efficiency and focus. They also bring a sense of well-being to a space.

Red is active and "passion-inspiring."[2] While this color can rev up a person's heart rate and blood flow upon sight, in the long term, it may be too intense.

Yellow, viewed by some color psychologists as the shade of optimism, is considered energetic and fresh and believed to trigger creativity.[3]

Choose a color that works for you and makes you excited to come to work. I love dark, rich colors, so I went with a gray in my home office; it looks good with white trim, and with the vaulted ceilings and natural light it feels cozy and brings me a sense of power.

You may want to start by taking a stroll through your local paint store to look at different colors and test a few out. See what calls to you and makes you smile.

Photos

They say a picture is worth a thousand words. Pictures represent what is important to you; they can be photos of family and friends or even ones for inspiration such as places where you want to travel. They can also be a fantastic motivator!

I have a vision board that illustrates who I want to become, places I want to visit, and other goals I will accomplish. Surrounding myself with photos doesn't just excite me and bring me joy, it reminds me of what I am working toward. These photos are my rocket fuel and give me the energy to push forward and show up daily. I find that many of my clients and mentors create vision boards too. Here are some simple tips to help you create yours:

1. Get either a large corkboard or poster board. I like one that is about three feet by two feet.

2. Use the life list that you created in chapter 3 and then find photos, quotes, words, or anything else that helps represent the items you included on your list.

3. Place the items on your board. You can organize them by category, such as life, career, relationships, and health. Or you can be more free-flowing with it. Every year I begin by choosing a word of the year—a word that represents what I want to focus on. (As I'm writing this, my word is *believe.*) I like to put that word right in the center of my vision board and have all other items flow from that word.

Look at your vision board daily. The more you look at it, the more you will stay connected with your vision. Each time you look at it, those images imprint on your nonconscious brain. In her article "Seeing Is Believing: The Power of Visualization," A. J. Adams notes that "Brain studies now reveal that thoughts produce the same mental instructions as actions. Mental imagery impacts many cognitive processes in the brain: motor control, attention, perception, planning, and memory. So the brain is getting trained for actual performance during visualization."[4] When we tell our brain what we want, it has a way of making it happen.

Organization

You can create simple systems in your work area to help keep you on track and focused. Have a system for filing paperwork, working on projects, and putting important dates on the calendar. One of my favorite things to do is writing notes by hand. I know it's old-fashioned and takes time, but I find most recipients are deeply touched by my effort and it is a great way to show my value to them both on a personal and professional level. My system includes having a box of note cards and stamps readily available, plus my favorite pens and access to all my addresses. This system makes it easy to complete my notes on a daily basis so I do not fall behind.

Personal effects

Make your workspace *yours* with other personal effects. You spend a lot of time in your space so you should create one that makes you feel welcomed, inspired, and joyful. Maybe you have a favorite lamp or paperweight on your desk, or maybe a plant. I have a bookshelf with reading materials I can grab and reflect on daily, as well as a rug from my parents' house and some other fun knickknacks.

Because your environment plays a huge role in your success, it should be designed with that success in mind. You should not only enjoy being in your space, but it should also feed your creativity and energy. A great place to brainstorm is Pinterest; you can search "home office" or "office space ideas," and hundreds of ideas will pop up for you to look through. You can look at colors, décor, and styles. In addition, you can also pull up pictures or inspirational words that you may want to hang on the wall or put on your vision board.

YOUR CIRCLE

We become who we spend time with, so we need to be aware of who is in our circle. This relates to our biological need for belonging. Many have noted that our need to belong is inherent in humans. In her book *The Psychology of Belonging*, Kelly-Ann Allen writes that:

> Belonging to groups, whether these be families, groups of friends, social groups, schools, workplaces, or communities more broadly, has a positive effect on several key factors that contribute to our successful healthy functioning as human beings in a society.
>
> We (humans) find much of our meaning, identity, relevance, and satisfaction in life through our sense of belonging to groups. At family, community, and societal levels, we rely on others for support, validation, and understanding.[5]

I believe that besides food, clothing, and shelter, connection and belonging is a basic human need we all crave and seek. Connection to others allows us to not just find "home" and a wholeness, but it gives us a sense of acceptance, love, happiness, and fulfillment. Academically, belonging is defined as "a unique and subjective experience that relates to a yearning for connection with others, the need for positive regard, and the desire for interpersonal connection."[6]

As Canadian author Toko-pa Turner writes, "at the very heart of 'belonging' is the word 'long.' To be-long to something is to stay with it for the long haul. It is an active choice we make to a relationship, to a place, to our body, to a life because we value it."[7]

We can get this sense of belonging in many ways. We can certainly spend more time with our friends and family, we can join networking groups (online or in person), or we can become part of a club/church/ organization. And it is also important to note that connection doesn't mean you need to immerse yourself in a large group; connection can be found simply with one other person.

Since we are talking about connecting with others, I want to point out that people can be like either a steam engine or an anchor—one can help us go forward and the other can hold us back. In looking at the path to success, we need to be cautious of ones that can hold us back.

Your associates

At a seminar I attended, the speaker talked about three groups of people: those we are associated with, those we have limited associations with, and those we are not associated with. You want to spend most of your time with the people in the first group; these are the individuals you may look to for accountability, mentorship, motivation, and overall skill building. They either are on a similar path to success or possibly have achieved success in a way that inspires you to be more like them. They are positive, driven, and support you on your journey to transformation. You may know them personally or simply via technology; I do not know some of my associates personally, but I spend time with them regularly through podcasts, reading, and watching them speak.

Here are some examples of people you may associate with regularly:

- Friends: people you enjoy spending time with. They can bring you laughter and share your pain and sadness. With this group you are 100 percent accepted for who you are, no judgment or need to be false or unauthentic.

- Mentors: people who will help you grow. You can learn from them, brainstorm with them, and feel safe asking them for help. I have had mentors throughout my life and career. They have helped me to work smarter, be more purposeful, and cut my learning curve dramatically.

- Strategic partners: people that you can connect with in an effort to grow your business and reach a greater level of success. They may help you host client events, promote your work, connect you to others, or work with you on specific projects. My strategic partners include other coaches and speakers. We can collaborate together and also refer clients to one another so we can all serve our clients and grow our businesses.

OUTSIDE SOURCES

You can also find connection in a more passive way. For example,

- Books: Throughout history, books have been a valuable resource to both teach and connect. Have you ever gotten "lost" in a book? Became so invested in the topic that you lost track of time? That is connection; you became a part of that book.

- Podcasts: The age of technology has allowed us to connect, learn, and grow through podcasts. Every day, podcasters are sharing interviews, humor, stories, and tips on every topic from parenting to business. When you follow a podcast, you become part of that community, and often they have other online groups and chat rooms to meet other listeners and share ideas.

- Classes: Like books, taking classes has proven successful over time. Now you can not only attend a live, in-person class, but you can also choose from thousands of classes to take online. You have the ability to take a class alongside people from other countries and other walks of life. It is truly an amazing way to learn. When I was getting my master's degree in organizational communications and leadership, I had several online classes that allowed me to meet and work with others from Alaska, California, and New York, while I was located in Colorado.

Creating an environment both physical and personal that will allow you to grow and thrive is a key to your success as a Mompreneur. Life is too important to live it alone. Now with so many avenues and ways to connect, you can not only stay close to your local circle, but also dive into any number of online opportunities. Get started today on building an environment and circle that will move you forward and help you accomplish greatness.

ACTION STEPS

1. List one thing you can change in your environment to help support you as a Mompreneur:

_____

_____

_____

_____

2. List three people you feel can help support you
   the most:

   _____

   _____

   _____

3. Find one group you can join to support you and
   allow you to connect:

   _____

   _____

   _____

4. Biggest aha moment from this chapter:

   _____

   _____

   _____

   _____

   _____

11

DEVELOPING A
PURPOSE-DRIVEN WEEK

Success doesn't come from what you do occasionally.
It comes from what you do consistently.

—MARIE FORLEO

One of the questions clients ask most often ask me is "How do I do it all?" Well, the answer is *you don't*.

We've already talked about how Mompreneurs can't do it all and the importance of setting boundaries and saying no. But regardless that still leaves a lot for us to get done. So what's the best way to do that? We have to make choices. We must shift our focus from doing it all to doing the *right* things.

The only way to get it all done is to take an honest look at:

- What needs to get done

- What needs to get done by *you*
- What others can do for you
- How to schedule with purpose

What do I mean by an honest look? I think we can be our biggest critics and biggest obstacles. Mompreneurs tend to go into the week with the intention of being Superwoman and getting it all done, when the reality is, we cannot. We need to start being honest about what we can realistically handle. We need to set ourselves up for success instead of overwhelming ourselves.

The first thing you need to be honest about is time. How much time do you really have to dedicate to work each week? Some weeks you will have the full effort, and other weeks, that is simply not the case.

One of my clients came to me feeling shame and failure because she had completed only a few tasks on her to-do list. She felt as if she had "wasted" the day.

When we talked about her day, it became clear what had happened.

She had woken up, taken her daughter to the orthodontist, met a client, worked on a report, and driven her other daughter to soccer practice at 3:00 p.m. When we went over these items, we realized she actually did *not* waste any time. You see, in truth, while she put in only about a three-hour workday instead of a full eight hours, in those three hours she did, in fact, *work*.

The problem was she was not honest about her available time as she went into the day. She set her day up with the mindset that it was going to be a normal eight- to nine-hour day, and when she didn't work those full hours, she determined that she had failed. If she had instead started the morning with honesty and realistically looked at the requirements of her schedule, she would have seen that it would not be a normal day, but only a three-hour workday. When viewed through this more accurate lens, she was not a failure at all but rather quite purposeful.

When she was able to see this, she felt better and learned a valuable lesson. Set your schedule with purpose for each specific day. Make the needed adjustments and realize it is not the hours that count but how you use those hours.

When you become clear about the actual time you have to work each day, it will be much easier to then determine what you need to focus on and what others can hold you accountable for.

PLAN YOUR WEEK

In chapter 5, you learned about creating a weekly plan. For a quick review, here are the key steps to preparing a weekly plan: 1) reflect on the prior week, 2) game-plan the upcoming week, and 3) put your schedule together. We're going to focus on steps 2 and 3 so you can start putting this weekly plan to work for yourself. (You can find a template in the Appendix.)

When you game-plan for your week, you are taking time to assess all the things, personal- and business-related, you need to address, including necessary meetings and calls, important dates and deadlines, appointments, project or client work, family time, self-care time, even errands or other miscellaneous items that you want to get done.

By clearly laying out your targets for the week, you gain clarity on where your focus and energy need to go and on which days. You can then use this information to put your detailed schedule together. After you create your targets, you then need to (again) be honest with your available time for the week and start to block out time for the things that will help you achieve your goals.

Time-block your calendar

How many hours are you available for the week? What are your hours of operation?

If you have personal tasks such as doctor appointments, school meetings, and family events, block these times out as unavailable, so you are sure to not include that time as available work time. After all, you are *not* available during these times.

Next, schedule your life. This is *key*. Part of being successful is making sure you are living your life. We know that the things that get scheduled get done, so make sure to schedule time for living. These include items like:

- Working out
- Self-care
- Days off
- Vacation

Work to *live*, don't live to work.

Last, time-block for your Vital Few items related to your business.

Now you have your week together. You have identified when you are working and when you are off, you have carved out time for your core fundamental activities, and what you have left is your available time, which you can fill with your other duties.

And remember: You *can* change and alter your schedule when it makes good business sense.

YOUR VITAL FEW

In chapter 5 we defined and discussed the importance of the Vital Few. Let's take a closer look at how identifying and then working on them can truly transform your week, and take you from being reactive to becoming a Mompreneur with purpose.

About three years ago I worked with Margo. She is amazing! She had been successful in her business for nine years but was struggling with maintaining consistency and not getting pulled off her schedule. Like many working moms, she juggled three children, a wonderful husband, and a thriving business. As we began to work together, the main thing we focused on was her weekly plan. This was something she had never considered prior to our working together. We began by clearly identifying her goals and vision and then connecting the best actions (her Vital Few) that would get her to her goals. After this it was simply a matter of helping her create a schedule that made sense and worked for her. What happened? Within six months of following her weekly plan, her business increased by 136 percent, and it continued to climb over the next several years.

By simply focusing on her Vital Few, she was able to control her days, get clear on her best and most productive actions, and still have room to live her life. That is the power of creating a weekly plan around your core activities.

For my Vital Few, I identified the core fundamentals that I need to do to create both the business and personal life I desire:

- My morning routine. This includes mindset work like affirmations and gratitude practice, working out, looking over my schedule for the day, and coffee.

- Handwritten notes. I love this practice and it has had a strong impact on my business.

- Face-to-face meeting. I work to have at least one face-to-face meeting with someone on my target list.

- Personal development. I spend about forty-five to sixty minutes a day growing myself and my skills.

- Social media. I write two blog posts a week and also daily posts to social media to be both visible and a valuable resource to my target audience.

- Write. I write for at least fifteen minutes a day.

- Calls. I make calls to potential clients as well as others I have done business with to stay connected and maintain relationships.

- Create my weekly plan.

I know that when I do these items consistently, I will connect with the right people, adding value to my target audience and building relationships that will result in business down the road.

Once you have identified your Vital Few, put those into your schedule and time-block around them; these items now become appointments. We show up for our appointments and we need to make sure we are showing up for our Vital Few.

WHAT SHOULD I DO? WHAT SHOULD I NOT DO?

As women in business, we often equate success with doing it all, which is both backward and wrong. We actually can accomplish more by doing less.

We need to become better at focusing on doing the right things for ourselves in our designated role and delegating things that are better completed by others. Here are some questions to help you determine what you should do and what can be delegated to others:

1. What do you enjoy doing? What brings you joy?

   We will never love all parts of our job, but when we can spend most of our time doing the tasks that bring us joy, we will accomplish them quicker, with more accuracy and find more contentment. The parts of my job that bring me joy are content creation, writing, and teaching. I also love to be creative. Some Mompreneurs prefer to delegate tasks such as writing blogs or doing social media posts; I, however, really enjoy those tasks as doing them feeds my creativity and allows me to be productive. On the flip side, I do not enjoy administrative tasks such as billing, formatting documents, and editing; it is better for me to delegate those tasks to someone else.

2. What is your role in your organization?

   You want to make sure you are doing what is required of your position in your company. If your primary role is leadership, you should not focus your time on lower-level management or administrative tasks. For example, one of my clients has a small contracting company; it is her role to oversee projects, generate new business, and keep the clients happy. She focuses on those priorities and has an accountant who watches the bottom line, a marketing person to direct the advertising, and an assistant to manage her schedule.

3. Is there someone else better qualified to handle this task?

   As previously discussed, you do not have to do it all and sometimes there is another party that is better able to handle certain tasks. You need to focus on your circle of control and let others around you do the same. For example, with the real estate professionals who I work with, I encourage them to delegate lending issues to those experts instead of handling it themselves.

In the end, everything you do comes down to these three points:

1. If you don't like it, don't do it.

2. If it is not in your wheelhouse, make it someone else's responsibility.

3. If someone has more control over a specific task, let them handle it.

No one has ever said that *you* have to do it all. We have created that mantra all on our own—but we can also change that mantra. It is not about doing it all; it is about doing the right things and doing them at an extraordinary level.

Success lies in being purposeful and not reactive. Follow these tips and you will be able to design a purpose-driven week during which you can focus on fewer items at a higher level and deliver the excellence you know you can. As a result, your clients, your family, and *you* will be happier and more productive.

ACTION STEPS

1. List your Vital Few or core weekly activities:

_____

_____

_____

_____

_____

2. Write down what brings you joy in the work you do:

_____

_____

_____

_____

_____

3. Write down your primary role in your organization/ company:

_____

_____

_____

_____

4. List what items you do not enjoy and who can help you with those:

_____

_____

_____

_____

_____

5. Biggest aha moment from this chapter:

_____

_____

_____

_____

_____

CONCLUSION

Being a working mom is hard, and it is also wonderful.

I was watching a television show in which the mom (a successful Mompreneur) was having a conversation with her daughter about having kids. The daughter commented on how hard it looked, and she made the statement to her mom, "You tried so hard and made mistakes! I am a mess so I don't even know how I stand a chance!" And her mother calmly replied, "You will mess up. It is inevitable. And it is also worth it."

Being a Mompreneur is not about being perfect. It is about being perfectly im-perfect. It's about showing up, being present, doing your best, acknowledging your shortcomings, asking for help, and granting yourself kindness. No one gets out of this life without making mistakes. The mistakes do not matter; what matters is what we learn from them and how we go forward.

I have learned a lot on my journey, and those lessons came from a lot of mistakes. There were times I thought I had it all together, and other times I could not have felt like more of a failure. I have had some *huge* mom failures, including:

- missing my son's eighth-grade graduation
- yelling when I didn't mean to
- being late for a pickup
- burning cookies
- falling asleep watching movies

But in the end, I found my way. Here are some of my favorite lessons learned:

- Be true to yourself.
- Say no when you want to.
- Ask for what you need.
- Be honest with yourself and others.
- Be the best you can be—even if the best that day is a hot mess.

The biggest takeaway I hope that you as a Mompreneur find, though, is that you can do this—you *can* create success in business and also as a mom. There is harmony and light in it all. But you must create your path on your terms. Stop living for others and trying to be what "they" think you should be and just be *you*.

You are amazing.

We have enough forces working against us. Stand tall in your vision. You know what you need and what is best for you. It is OK if others do not see it yet—they will. And in the end simply ask yourself, "Am I proud of who I have become?"

Much love and appreciation to all of you working moms. You got this!

Your cheerleader,

Clara

ACKNOWLEDGMENTS

This book would not have happened without the support and guidance of many people. To start with, my parents. They always supported me and my crazy ideas. They would challenge me and encourage me to fight for what I wanted. And when I wanted to give up (which happened a lot), they would not let me. It was my mom who convinced me to leave my corporate job and find my true calling; her encouragement and support allowed me to feel confident to go after my dreams, even as a single mom.

My son, Nicholas—after all, he made me a mom. Being on the road was not always easy. I missed time with him and events like sports and even eighth-grade graduation. But he always loved me and told me it was OK.

My mentors Larry Kendall, Karen Ricci, and Steve Salinas, and all of my Ninja family gave me the courage to know that my vision matters and that my story needs to be told. Whenever I have questions, feel lost, or need encouragement, they are there for me cheering me on.

And to all the other working moms I meet—you are more than you think you are. You walk with grace, heart, and spirit. And even when you think you are failing, you are not. Keep following your path. Be honest. Be authentic. Be you.

APPENDIX:
MY FAVORITE THINGS

My success didn't come on its own; I had help. There are many resources I relied on that provided guidance and value. Here are a few:

BOOKS:

Mindset, Carol Dweck (Ballantine Books)

Ninja Selling, Larry Kendall (Greenleaf Book Group Press)

The Go-Giver, Bob Burg and John David Mann (Portfolio/Penguin)

The *School of Greatness*, Lewis Howes (Rodale)

The *Slight Edge*, Jeff Olson with John David Mann (Greenleaf Book Group Press)

PODCASTS:

Smartless, with Jason Bateman, Sean Hayes, and Will Arnett, https://www.smartless.com

On Purpose, with Jay Shetty, https://jayshetty.me/podcast/

WEBSITES:

Robin Sharma, https://www.robinsharma.com

WEEKLY SUCCESS PLANNER

Date: _____

Review of Last Week:

On a scale of 1 to 10, how did last week go? _____

What could you have done differently to make it closer to a 10?

_____

_____

_____

Tracking:

Virtual Coffee: _____

New Leads: _____

Cold Calls Made: _____

Connection Calls Made: _____

New Clients: _____

Hours Worked: _____

PLAN FOR THIS WEEK:

What strategic partners, communities, clients will you reach out to?

_____

_____

_____

Who do you need to follow up with (leads, contacts, people)?

_____

_____

_____

What projects do you need to work on?

_____

_____

_____

What meetings or calls do you have scheduled?

_____

_____

_____

Other:

_____

_____

_____

Is your schedule put together? _____

How many hours will you work this week? _____

Do you have time blocked for your Vital Few
(reach-outs, business development, posts, etc.)? _____

Do you have personal time scheduled?

_____

_____

_____

_____

_____

What roadblocks, if any, do you anticipate?

_____

_____

_____

_____

_____

What do you need help with? Who can help you?

_____

_____

_____

_____

_____

30-DAY SUCCESS STRATEGY PLAN

Month: _____

What is your annual goal? $ _____

Current YTD income earned: $ _____

What was the BEST thing that happened in your business last month?

_____

_____

_____

_____

What, if anything, was a missed opportunity?

_____

_____

_____

_____

How could you have approached it differently?

_____

_____

_____

_____

Business:

30-day targets   **Key action steps to get you there**

#1 _____   _____

#2 _____   _____

What are three resources that can help you
(classes, people, books, etc.)?

_____

_____

_____

Who can hold you accountable?
Affirmation:

_____

_____

_____

_____

90-DAY ACTION PLAN

Quarter: _____

YTD Income: _____

YTD Goal: _____

What worked best for my business last quarter?

_____

_____

_____

_____

What is an area/system that needs improvement?

_____

_____

_____

_____

How can I improve this?

_____

_____

_____

_____

_____

Goals for the next 90 days:

      Income: _____

      Personal: _____

What five Actions will be BEST for me to achieve these goals?

Income	Personal
_____	_____
_____	_____
_____	_____
_____	_____
_____	_____

What resources do I need to help me?

_____

_____

_____

_____

_____

What skill set do I want to focus on this quarter?

_____

_____

_____

_____

_____

Who/what can help me?

_____

_____

_____

_____

_____

What do I need to stop doing so I can make time for the right actions?

_____

_____

_____

_____

_____

PERFECT DAY TRACKER

Perfect Day Tracker Master

Name: Clara
Month: June 2022

Gauges: Retail, Recruiting, Retention

Personal Volume Goal: ___ Monthly Distributor Goal: ___
New Customer Goal: ___ Event Guest Goal: ___

Action	Target	1	2	3	4	5	6	7	8	9	10	11	12	13	14	15	16	17	18	19	20	21	22	23	24	25	26	27	28	29	30	31	TOTAL
DMO & Gauges																																	
1) 30 min reachouts and connections																1	1	1	1	1	1	1											
2) Social Media Posts																1	1	1	1	1	1												2
3) Discovery Cal																	2																
4) Virtual Coffee/Meet and Greet Call																1	1	1	1	1													5
5) Lead Follow Up																1	1	1	1	1	1												5
6) Speaking /Podcast Applications																					2												0
Success Habits																																	
Wake up / Morning Routine	1 Point															1	1	1	1	1													4
Personal Development /Mindset	1 Point															1	1	1	1	1	1												5
Workout	1 Point															1	1	1	1	1													5
Relationships	1 Point															1	1	1	1	1	1												
Daily Total	5 Points	0	0	0								0	0	0	0	9	9	6	6	8	7	0	0	0	0	0	0	0	0	0	0	0	45
Discovery Call booked																																	
Sales (Capano)																	2																2
Sales (Ninja)																																	
Bookings (free like Summits and Podcasts)		1					1																										

NOTES

CHAPTER 1

1. John Assaraf and Murray Smith, *The Answer: Grow Any Business, Achieve Financial Freedom, and Live an Extraordinary Life* (New York: Atria Books, 2008).

2. Geoffrey L. Cohen and David K. Sherman, "The Psychology of Change: Self-Affirmation and Social Psychological Intervention," *Annual Review of Psychology*, no. 65 (January 2014): 333–371, https://www.annualreviews.org/doi/abs/10.1146/annurev-psych-010213-115137.

3. Carol S. Dweck, *Mindset: The Psychology of Success* (New York: Random House, 2006).

CHAPTER 3

1. *Oxford English Dictionary* (2001), s.v. "vision."

2. John Kotter, *Leading Change* (Boston: Harvard Business School Press, 1996), 67–84.

3. Jim Collins and Jerry Porras, "Building Your Company's Vision," *Harvard Business Review*, September–October 1996.

CHAPTER 4

1. Clara Capano, "The Power of Boundaries and Stepping into Growth," March 18, 2021, in *The Working Woman's Channel*, Season 2, episode 1, 23:01, https://www.youtube.com/watch?v=o59dIXVm1-Y.

2. Lee Cockerell, *Creating Magic: 10 Common Sense Leadership Strategies from a Life at Disney* (New York, NY: Doubleday, 2008).

3. Mel Robbins, *The 5 Second Rule: Transform Your Life, Work, and Confidence with Everyday Courage* (Houston, TX: Savio Republic, 2017).

CHAPTER 5

1. Ira E. Hyman Jr. et al., "Did You See the Unicycling Clown? Inattentional Blindness while Walking and Talking on a Cell Phone," *Applied Cognitive Psychology* 24, no. 5 (2009): 597–607, accessed December 17, 2020. DOI: 10.1002/acp.1638.

2. Hyman, "Did You See."

3. Luke Seavers, *Time-Blocking* (One Nine Pro Publishing, January 2, 2021).

4. Michael Hyatt and Daniel Harkavy, *Living Forward: A Proven Plan to Stop Drifting and Get the Life You Want* (Grand Rapids, MI: Baker Books, 2016).

5. Stephen R. Covey, "Big Rocks," *FranklinCovey*, 1994, https://resources. franklincovey.com/the-8th-habit/big-rocks-stephen-r-covey.

6. Laura Vanderkam, *168 Hours: You Have More Time Than You Think* (New York: Portfolio, 2010).

CHAPTER 6

1. Arianna Huffington, *The Sleep Revolution: Transforming Your Life, One Night at a Time* (New York: Harmony Books, 2016).

2. Stephen J. Bronner, "Strategy: Should You Tell People About Your Goals, or Keep Them a Secret?" *Inverse*, March 4, 2020, https://www.inverse.com/ innovation/should-you-share-your-goals-heres-what-science-has-to-say.

3. Arianna Huffington, *The Sleep Revolution* (New York: Harmony, 2016).

4. D. Hillman, S. Mitchell, J. Streatfeild, C. Burns, D. Bruck, and L. Pezzullo, "The Economic Cost of Inadequate Sleep," *Sleep* 41, no. 8 (August 2018).

5. M. L. Haavisto, T. Porkka-Heiskanen, C. Hublin, M. Harma, P. Mutanan, K. Muller et al., "Sleep Restriction for the Duration of a Work Week Impairs Multitasking Performance," *Journal of Sleep Research* 19, no. 3 (September 2010): 444–54, https://doi.org/10.1111/ j.1365-2869.2010.00823.x.

6. C. M. Barnes, C. L. Guarana, S. Nauman, and D. T. Kong, "Too Tired to Inspire or Be Inspired: Sleep Deprivation and Charismatic Leadership," *Journal of Applied Psychology* 101, no. 8 (August 2016): 1191, https://doi.org/10.1037/apl0000123.

7. U. John, C. Meyer, H. J. Rumpf, and U. Hapke, "Relationships of Psychiatric Disorders with Sleep Duration in an Adult General Population Sample," *Journal of Psychiatric Research* 39 (2005): 577e83; N. F. Watson, K. P. Harden, D. Buchwald, M. V. Vitiello, A. L. Pack, E. Strachan et al., "Sleep Duration and Depressive Symptoms: A Gene-Environment Interaction," *Sleep* 37 (2014): 351e8; J. C. Kearns, D. D. L. Coppersmith, A. C. Santee, C. Insel, W. R. Pigeon, C. R. Glenn, "Sleep Problems and Suicide Risk in Youth: A Systematic Review, Developmental Framework, and Implications for Hospital Treatment," *General Hospital Psychiatry* 63 (March–April 2020): 141–151.

8. For more information on the importance of naps, see: Tom Barlow, "Nap Your Way to Success," *Forbes*, May 17, 2011, https://www.forbes.com/sites/tombarlow/2011/05/17/nap-your-way-to-success/?sh=18bb198421d3.

CHAPTER 7

1. "What is DiSC?" DiSC Profile, https://www.discprofile.com/what-is-disc.

2. Marianne Williamson, *A Return to Love* (New York: HarperPerennial, 1993), 191.

3. Tanvi Akhauri, "Are Women Bigger People Pleasers Than Men?" Shethepeople.tv, July 12, 2021.

CHAPTER 9

1. Wendy Wood, Jeffrey M. Quinn, and Deborah A. Kashy, "Habits in Everyday Life: Thought, Emotion, and Action," *Journal of Personality and Social Psychology* 83 (2002): 1281–87.

2. Wood, Quinn, and Kashy, "Habits in Everyday Life."

3. Nabil Alshurafa, Haik Kalantarian, Mohammad Pourhomayoun, Jason J. Liu, Shruti Sarin, Behnam Shahbazi, and Majid Sarrafzadeh, "Recognition of Nutrition Intake Using Time-Frequency Decomposition in a Wearable Necklace Using a Piezoelectric Sensor," *IEEE Sensors Journal* 17, no. 5 (July 2015): 3909–3916, https://doi.org/10.1109/JSEN.2015.2402652.

4. James Clear, *Atomic Habits: An Easy & Proven Way to Build Good Habits & Break Bad Ones* (New York: Avery, 2018).

5. Beata Souders, "The Vital Importance and Benefits of Motivation," *Positive Psychology*, November 5, 2019, https://positivepsychology.com/benefits-motivation.

6. C. Peterson, S. F. Maier, and M. E. P. Seligson, *Learned Helplessness: A Theory for the Age of Personal Control* (New York: Oxford University Press, 1993).

7. "Accountability partners and why you need one," Signature Analytics, accessed March 2022, https://signatureanalytics.com/blog/accountability-partners-and-why-you-need-one/.

CHAPTER 10

1. Nancy Kwallek, "Work Week Productivity, Visual Complexity, and Individual Environmental Sensitivity in Three Offices of Different Color Interiors," *Color Research & Application* 32, no. 2 (April 2007): 130–143, https://www.researchgate.net/publication/229586737_Work_week_productivity_visual_complexity_and_individual_environmental_sensitivity_in_three_offices_of_different_color_interiors.

2. Kim Lachance Shandrow, "How the Color of Your Office Impacts Productivity," *Entrepreneur*, March 9, 2015, https://www.entrepreneur.com/living/how-the-color-of-your-office-impacts-productivity/243749.

3. Shandrow, "Color of Your Office."

4. A. J. Adams, "Seeing Is Believing: The Power of Visualization," *Psychology Today*, December 3, 2009, https://www.psychologytoday.com/us/blog/flourish/200912/seeing-is-believing-the-power-visualization.

5. Kelly-Ann Allen, *The Psychology of Being* (New York: Routledge, 2021).

6. Carl Rogers, *Client-Centered Therapy: Its Current Practice, Implications, and Theory* (Boston: Houghton Mifflin, 1951).

7. Toko-pa Turner, *Belonging: Remembering Ourselves Home* (Salt Spring Island, British Columbia: Her Own Room Press, 2017).

INDEX

ABOUT THE AUTHOR

Clara Capano is an international speaker, trainer, and best-selling author. She is also the creator and host of *The Working Woman's Channel* and *Living Real TV.* After years of chasing success and happiness, she realized that the only way to truly achieve her "dream" life was to redefine what success was for her. Her journey led her to find CLARATY and create a life she loves on her terms. She now spends her time speaking and working with women across the globe to help them lean into their greatness and create their own paths to CLARATY.

Clara is the mother to her amazing son, Nicholas, and dog, Lulu. When not working, she enjoys travel, food, and spending time at the beach.